IGOR
The Courage of Chernobyl's Child

For Dr Tamara Mourashova and Lilya Greenhouse,
who did so much for Igor in his early years

For Victor, whose tenacity and kindness gives hope
to the courageous children of Chernobyl

And for Barbara and Roy Bennett, who have given Igor
a home

IGOR
The Courage of Chernobyl's Child

By Jane Warren

BOXTREE

First published in Great Britain in 1996 by Boxtree Limited,
Broadwall House, 21 Broadwall, London SE1 9PL

Copyright © 1996 Jane Warren
Illustrations copyright © Igor Pavlovets
All rights reserved

ISBN: 0 7522 0354 1

A CIP catalogue entry for this book is available from the
British Library.

Typeset by SX Composing DTP, Rayleigh, Essex
Printed and bound in Great Britain by The Bath Press

Contents

Acknowledgements

With huge thanks to Richard Compton Miller, without whom this book could not have happened.

I must also thank Valentina Chakhlai for her help in finding the answers to obscure questions and translating from Russian to English; Bob Taylor and Alan Stephenson of Hugh Steeper Ltd; the government of the Republic of Belarus; the Embassy of the Republic of Belarus in London; the British Embassy in Minsk; the Rt Hon. Michael Howard, QC, MP; the Rt Hon. Virginia Bottomley, MP, and her assistant, Mrs Glennie; Norm Abl and Wendy Sethi of Austrian Airlines; *Express Newspapers*; Vincent Tucker; Sue Reid; Maria Obrasova; the Chernobyl Children Life Line links; Birgitta Mizzi for warmth and nourishment; Andrea Boulter for crucial legal support; Sara Browne; Zenith North; Alan Frame and Kim Willsher; and Robert and Louise Mayhew.

Particular credit is due to Adrian Sington, Naia Bray-Moffatt and their colleagues at Boxtree for having the flair to produce this book in just two months from commission.

Finally, a special thank-you to my wonderfully supportive mother Susan Warren and my friend Clare Minting for their insightful suggestions; to technical consultant Quentin King for helping to make complex information both user-friendly and accurate; and to my junior proof-readers, Joanna and Chloë Nahum-Claudel.

Foreword

by the Rt Hon. Virginia Bottomley, MP

I am only too conscious of the anxiety suffered by parents who look after handicapped children, and of their grief when their children are ill. Jane Warren's moving book tells the inspiring story of Igor Pavlovets, born with terrible deformities as a consequence of the Chernobyl disaster ten years ago. Igor's mother felt she had no option but to give him away, because she couldn't cope.

I have met children from the region near Chernobyl on many occasions and have always been impressed by their behaviour and courage. Among them, Igor stands out. His spirited cheerfulness is an inspiration to us all. Igor was born with few advantages, but has overcome his predicament in a way which could melt the frostiest heart. He is able to lead a normal life and take part in all the activities children enjoy, and always with such enthusiasm.

The people who undertake the responsibility of helping such children are worthy of the highest praise. Many people have good intentions, but families who open their home, as Roy and Barbara Bennett have done for Igor, are examples to us all. I am proud that a British charity was able to see his potential. Without the intervention of Chernobyl Children Life Line, Igor would still be living in an institution with no prospect of a future. The charity does tremendous work in helping the unfortunate children of the Republic of Belarus, which received 70 per cent of the contamination after the disaster. It has helped to create a better understanding between our society and theirs, and given a ray of hope to this stricken region.

I know Igor will do well in life. His courage and his personality will see him through the difficult years yet to come. Yet
his presence will always remind us of this terrible calamity and
of the importance of trying to leave our children a better, safer
world.

The House of Commons, March 1996

Prologue: The Cartwheel

It was Igor's first day at school. He was shrieking with laughter at the far end of the playground and cleverly dodging the other children who were trying to catch him. Out of the corner of his eye he could see Mrs Reid preparing to raise her hand to signal the end of break and the end of his game.

Igor Pavlovets was seven years old and a pupil of Badshot Lea County Infant School in Surrey, England. The teacher's arm shot into the air like a flag-pole. The other children ran over to queue patiently next to her. Igor stayed on the far side of the playground. Choosing his moment carefully, he took a deep breath and set off on a sequence of magnificent one-handed cartwheels across the width of the tarmac. The other children froze in amazement as he propelled his agile little body with his powerful arm. They broke into laughter and clapped their hands as the schoolboy acrobat bounced on to his feet and waved, before zooming into line with them. Igor bellowed with laughter and basked in the attention. All the children adored him, he was so cheerful and happy. A little ray of athletic magic had lit up the morning.

But Igor doesn't look like other children. When you first meet him, it is as if his body has been chopped off in the middle. He is only as tall as a toddler. He has no hips and where his thighs should be are two strange feet, bent back on themselves like flippers of muscle. They are both turned out, pointing sideways. Igor's left arm, his muscular cartwheel arm, is perfectly formed, but he doesn't have a right arm at all. If you saw him swimming, you'd notice just a tiny mound of muscle near his right shoulder. It looks as if his arm has been

1

cleanly sliced off with a sword. Inside his custom-built shoes are more puzzles. His left foot has only two extra-long toes. Without his sock, the foot looks just like a fishtail. His right foot is missing two toes. But his deformities are all on the outside. Igor is a sunny boy with a glorious smile. He is also extremely intelligent.

Igor was born like this. His deformities were caused by the world's worst nuclear accident, which took place some 1,600 kilometres (1,000 miles) away from this suburban English scene. This wasn't the explosion of an atomic bomb, but a major disaster at a nuclear power plant in the former Soviet Union which happened on 26 April 1986.

What happened inside Chernobyl reactor number four at 1.23am on 26th April 1986

5. Radioactive debris scattered over one mile

6. Radioactive cloud spreads North West

4. Hydrogen mixes with air and explodes

3. Gas pressure blows top off core

2. Chemical reaction between water and graphite produces hydrogen gas and core heats up

1. Cooling water leaks into graphite core

H2O

CORE

Chapter 1 The Disaster

There was already a fire in the core of the reactor and flames were licking the roof like angry tongues when the phone shrilled at the home of Leonid, the nuclear reactor's fire chief. It was the control room, ringing in desperation. Leonid glanced at his clock: 1.25 a.m. He scrambled out of bed and pulled back the curtains. There was an orange glow across the rye and flax fields. Reactor number four at the Chernobyl power plant, a towering structure of concrete and steel, had seemed invulnerable but now the fire had taken hold and was lighting up the night sky.

Leonid grabbed his red helmet and leather gloves. He dressed quickly and, still doing up the brass buttons on his heavy grey coat, raced to the reactor, which was spitting fragments of metal and concrete from the roof. It was a warm spring night, made hotter by the boiling debris he was forced to dodge as he darted inside the power plant through the heavy door. He charged past the faded safety posters stuck on the walls along the endless concrete corridors, but he didn't notice them. Instead, his attention was focused on the smoke pouring from beneath the door of the reactor room. He turned the metal handle, pulled open the door and was almost knocked off his feet by a blast of boiling air. He shielded his eyes with his leather gloved hands and peered into the inferno, then ran to the corridor and phoned for assistance from other fire stations in the area. His team of twenty-eight men and three fire engines wasn't equipped to tackle this alone.

Leonid, who was in his thirties, knew that just by standing in the burning reactor he was gravely endangering his health, but he also knew that it was imperative to try to stop the fire spreading to one or more of the other three reactors. Each of them was the size of an aircraft carrier and the consequences of further explosions were too terrible to consider.

Leonid ran back outside. By now the area was crawling with poorly equipped fire trucks, all sounding their noisy klaxons. Their water jets were puny splashes against the white-hot inferno. They looked like crawling beetles next to the ugly sky-scraping walls. Leonid scrambled seventy metres (230 ft) up a metal ladder to the roof of the burning reactor to direct operations. By now, his fire crew were shouting to each other over the roar of the flames as they peered into the gaping mouth in the fractured roof. Completely dwarfed by the scale of the reactor, they were just tiny figures scurrying across the top of the flaming building, using picks and shovels to scrape fragments into the crater. Everything was confusion.

Smoke obscured the striped red and white chimney towering above the reactor and the soot made it difficult to breathe. Feeling his boots sticking to the roof, Leonid looked down at his feet. The black bitumen sealing the roof against the rain had melted because of the high temperatures and was starting to blister. He tore his feet from the gummy surface just in time. Moments after he began his hazardous descent from the roof, it collapsed completely. Flames leapt like rockets into the sky above the plant. Hundreds of smaller fires were ignited as burning debris and bitumen were thrown up and then smashed to the ground. Limbs of twisted metal were burning. Broken concrete lay in smoking boulders. Before the catastrophe, the most serious blaze Leonid had tackled was a peat fire in a local shop. But despite his inexperience, the brave fire chief and his men stayed on the front line to battle with the blaze. They worked on auto-pilot. This was their duty to their country, and to their wives and children still sleeping so close by. Even after they had put out the flames, however, the reactor would continue to smoulder for weeks.

Meanwhile, deep in the heart of the burning reactor, an engineer called Alexei was working feverishly in the control room. He had been there when the reactor exploded, after senior officers had ordered a precarious experiment to see if it could run on low power. They had shut off the safety systems and ignored the red alert and flashing lights. And now this: the core had become unstable and soared in temperature to 3,000 degrees centigrade, as hot as the molten heart of a volcano. The fuel pipes had buckled, causing an explosion of such force that it had blasted the lid off the reactor, killing several workers nearby.

Alexei began to press buttons to shut down the other three reactors. Like Leonid, he knew it was vital to do what he could to prevent another explosion, so he remained for four more hours. He concentrated hard, sweating with the effort of trying to bring the stricken reactor under control; it was like defusing a terrorists' time bomb. Soon he felt strangely unwell. Within the first two hours after the explosion, he had to rush out of the control room to be sick in the corridor, which was swirling with smoke. The fifty-five year-old understood the dangers and he knew that his nausea was the first symptom of massive radiation poisoning. The fire in the reactor's heart was pumping out a lethal cocktail of radioactive isotopes and to remain in the vicinity was to accept a death sentence, but he forced himself to ignore the signs. He had to leave the cooling systems for the other three reactors operational, otherwise they too could melt down and explode.

Once Alexei had made them as safe as he could, he raced out of the control room. Behind him, large portions of the walls of reactor number four were caving in. As he slammed the heavy metal door and ran out into the dawn sky towards his home, near Leonid's, Alexei had received three times the fatal dose of radiation. Feeling dizzy and weak, he looked up. A thick black cloud of smoke was stretching out from the reactor across the sky like a motorway. But instead of traffic, it was carrying 190 tonnes of lethal radioactive material out across the countryside.

Several hours after the meltdown, the area was swarming with thirty-seven fire brigades and a total of 186 firemen. The Soviet Minister for Energy had been told only of 'a small defect' at the reactor, which had been built to provide power for heavy industry such as refineries and metal foundries, but for nine days the invisible killer would silently pour forth from the crumbling reactor. Translated from Russian, Chernobyl means 'black truth', and the black truth of Chernobyl was radiation.

Most people never receive dangerously high doses of radiation in their lives. But if a nuclear reactor vessel is destroyed, huge quantities of radioactive fuel can escape and pollute the environment. Water, soil, plants and animals, including humans, will all absorb the contaminated material and living creatures will suffer as a result. The most frightening thing about radiation is that we have no senses to detect it. Neither sight, hearing, touch, taste nor smell will warn you of radiation, even fatal levels. You can't boil contaminated water or cook contaminated food to make it safe, and once radioactive isotopes are inside the body they will remain lodged in vital organs for decades, emitting radiation as they decay. This will corrupt the vital genetic code of cells. If the contamination is great enough, it is only a matter of time before a corrupted cell becomes cancerous, especially inside a child's body. And a field containing radioactive material will produce contaminated food for hundreds of years.

Nuclear power is supposed to be cheap to produce because the raw fuel is less expensive than oil or coal. But the rigorous safety requirements for operating a reactor and handling the spent fuel make it one of the most expensive sources of energy in the developed world. So the Soviets cut corners. Most of their reactors still have no safety shields. Neither do they have the right number of automatic shutdown systems that would operate in the event of disaster. The Soviets thought these were superfluous frills, and even mocked other countries for being over-cautious with their safety procedures. They boasted that their nuclear reactors were of a superior design, despite the fact that British experts had condemned reactors like the one at Chernobyl as unsafe thirty years before the disaster.

The local people didn't know any of this. All information about power plants in the Soviet Union was controlled by the secret police, who kept the real truth about Soviet nuclear power to themselves. So on the fateful night of the meltdown, the control-room staff who weren't directly involved with the experiment were probably dozing rather than watching their instruments. They had been led to believe that nothing could go wrong. They were told repeatedly during their training 'a nuclear power plant cannot explode'.

The first sign of impending disaster was probably a warning light. Winking on the control panel, it would have signalled that something was wrong with the water-cooling system. The Chernobyl style of nuclear reactor needed to have cold water pumped through its pipes so that it didn't overheat. But as the operators ignored the flashing light, water was actually seeping into the reactor's core. This rapidly turned into steam and a deadly chain reaction began. The temperature of the core soared and the huge vessel containing the core of the reactor erupted. An uprush of volatile hydrogen gas was released and ignited as it mixed with the air above the core. The roof was blown off the building and burning debris started fires. The experiment had run out of control and destroyed the reactor vessel, threatening millions of lives. But rather than admitting what had happened, the General Secretary of the Soviet Union, Mikhail Gorbachov, covered up details of the disaster. He didn't want the news to reach the outside world. But he couldn't hide the radiation. The day after the explosion, 1,300 kilometres (800 miles) north of the Chernobyl reactor, the Swedish government discovered huge levels of radiation during a routine air-quality check. Gorbachov was then forced to admit the problem to other governments, but he was vague, referring simply to 'a small accident'. He neglected to tell his own people anything; on the television and radio news there was barely a mention. Most people didn't realize how serious the situation was because everything was kept secret.

It took only hours for Alexei's radiation sickness to start. Soon his skin was itching and breaking into blisters which made him look as if he had run through fire. He had a sweet taste in his mouth, despite the fact he hadn't eaten for hours. Within days, his hair, like Leonid's, was falling out in clumps. Then he collapsed. Alexei was later driven to Moscow's City Hospital Six, where he was shrouded in a plastic sheet called a 'life island' that covered him from head to toe. His body was undergoing a total shutdown.

Radiation destroys the marrow at the heart of the bones so it can no longer produce new blood cells. There is also internal bleeding. The body's ability to fight off infection is wiped out, so even a cold or a minor scratch can prove fatal to someone who has absorbed too much radiation. From beneath the plastic, Alexei looked up at his wife and children when they came to visit him in hospital. They weren't allowed to touch him because his skin was so sore it would have made him cry out. They saw the visible signs of their father's poisoning under the hospital lights. All Alexei's hair had fallen out by now. His skin was a blotchy mahogany colour. But Alexei was calm, with the same stoic but frightened look of terminally ill cancer patients. When he died, he was a hero. A few weeks later Leonid, the brave fire chief, also died of radiation poisoning. Were it not for their efforts, the reactor core might have melted down even further and caused even greater devastation.

The government still hadn't admitted that there had been a disaster at Chernobyl. They hadn't revealed the truth about the fire still smouldering in the reactor, or that there was a molten lake of radioactive soup at its core, giving off a deadly vapour and urgently needing to be mopped up, or even that the land was slowly being poisoned by fall-out, the radioactive debris which drops from the sky and scatters over the ground after a nuclear explosion. So the children played happily outside during morning break without a clue of the dangers. Meanwhile, convoys of trucks had started streaming up and down the road to Chernobyl. When they got within thirty kilometres (20 miles) of the plant, they dumped their weighty deliveries of sand, cement and lead. The cargoes were then transferred to trucks already contaminated with radiation. These rumbled up the road to the plant, where the materials were once again off-loaded, this time to plug the boiling volcano.

Twenty-five Soviet helicopter pilots flew suicide missions 250 metres (800 ft) above the burning reactor. The aircraft looked like mechanical flies, dwarfed by the reactor. The pilots tried to dodge the plumes of dense radioactive smoke spewing into the sky. They flew in as low as they could to dive-bomb the burning reactor with sand to extinguish the fires or boron, a brown powder, to suppress the continuous nuclear reactions. The pilots had no anti-radiation suits to wear and had never tried to put out a nuclear fire before. All they could do was grab sheets of lead from the lorries and jam them on to the seats of their helicopters to act as feeble protection against the radiation shining out of the reactor. The pilots dumped so much sand as the weeks went by that American satellite pictures showed it spilling out all around the reactor. A new mission then had to begin to stop the reactor sinking through its foundations.

Initially, the pilots were working alongside ten robots lent by Germany and Japan. These robots shifted lumps of radioactive debris from the reactor's core and the roof, but they were soon useless. Radiation levels were so high that their circuits went haywire. They either raced out of control and slammed into walls or hurled themselves off the disintegrating roof. To replace them, Mikhail Gorbachov made a grim and calculated decision. He ordered the job to be finished by human hand. Teams of young men from all over the Soviet Union were ordered to do the work of the robots. Dressed in lead suits and glass visors, these 'bio-robots' began the laborious clean-up with shovels. They were just farmers, miners and factory workers, simple men who knew little of radiation but had the muscle power to work at speed. Their supervisors made a vain attempt to limit the men's exposure to levels of radiation which were so high that they could kill immediately. The men were given sixty seconds to rush up the ramp to the top of the reactor, grab a shovel and push two chunks of radioactive debris into the core. This was supposed to limit exposure to the most radioactively hot areas to five seconds.

They would also swarm around the base of the power plant, shovelling debris into piles and scooping it up into trucks, which would then drive to one of the 600 dumpsites within the contaminated zone to bury their radioactive load. Eventually the trucks themselves would be buried in these shallow graves. Piles of earth and stones were excavated at the sites, but because the job was done so quickly, they were neither deep enough nor well enough covered to be safe. The brave men, known as 'the liquidators', worked day and night to bury the crippled reactor itself. A vast army of over half a million men was conscripted to work at the disaster site over the coming year. The men were told that the faster they ran, the safer they would be, so they soon responded by shedding their lead trousers and aprons, which made it impossible to move, and got on with the deadly job as hastily as they could. They were then dressed only in thin white cotton overalls, which provided no protection, and cumbersome helmets which would mist up on the inside of the glass. They kept the helmets on because they were told that to breathe the vapour only briefly would kill them as quickly as a bullet.

All of them had soon received a lifetime's dose of radiation as they constructed a concrete sarcophagus over the top of the damaged reactor. To create the shroud, they used 6,000 tonnes of steel for the metal superstructure and coated it with a cement wall a metre thick. They hoped it would seal off the reactor and stop the radiation seeping into the atmosphere. They also scraped off the top twenty centimetres of soil from the area around the plant and replaced it with cement slabs. They chopped down forests of contaminated silver birch trees. They bulldozed farms and villages. Everything was badly buried by men who didn't understand the need for absolute precision. Yet Mikhail Gorbachov's government officials still insisted that radiation levels were low and everything was under control.

At night the brave liquidators slept in rest huts protected by solid layers of lead. They were given certificates from the government which proclaimed them to be heroes in the 'fight' against an 'enemy' called radiation. But the liquidators began to collapse. Hundreds have since died and thousands are seriously ill with terminal cancers. Despite the fact that the power station was a lethal zone, the government ferried in nuclear scientists from all over the Soviet Union to operate the three other reactors, which were soon restarted.

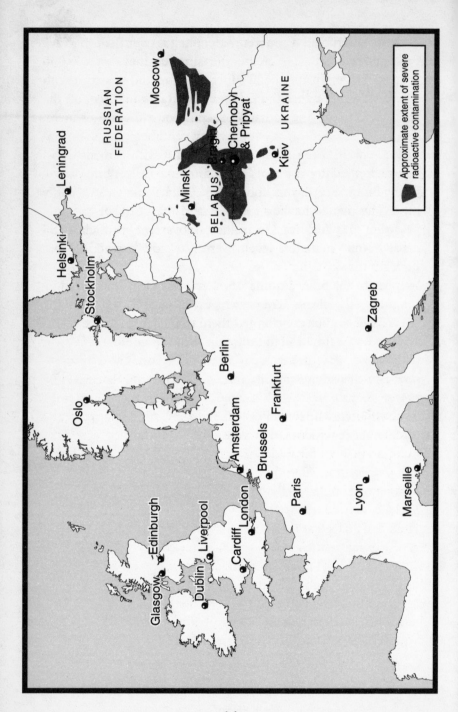

Approximate extent of severe radioactive contamination

RUSSIAN FEDERATION

Moscow

Leningrad

Helsinki

Stockholm

Oslo

Minsk

BELARUS

Bryan

Chernobyl & Pripyat

Kiev   UKRAINE

Berlin

Frankfurt

Amsterdam

Brussels

Zagreb

Paris

Lyon

Marseille

Edinburgh

Glasgow

Liverpool

Dublin

Cardiff

London

Chapter 2 The Evacuation

Just six hours after the explosion, children were waking up to an overcast Saturday morning in the Belarussian villages and towns. They would have had no idea of the overnight disaster. They were simply looking forward to a weekend spent playing in the forests. They got dressed and set out but something was wrong. In the sky a dark cloud cast a shadow over the cabbage and potato fields. A hostile wind scurried into eddies and whipped up the grass. And on the paths outside their houses, on the roads and in the playgrounds, a strange black dirt had settled. The air tasted of the ugly, gritty powder. The children didn't know what it was, so they decided it must be black snow. But this snow was different. It stained their hands and clothes.

The children who lived in the bustling town of Pripyat were in a state of excitement the morning after the reactor exploded. Their parents had forbidden them to go outside to play. They were among the 30,000 residents of the town which had sprung up a couple of kilometres from the Chernobyl reactor. Nearly a decade earlier, the engineers building the power station had arrived at the small pastoral community of wooden houses, bringing their wives and families. Shops had opened, schools were built and hospitals constructed. Gradually a prosperous town of high-rise apartment blocks had developed. It was a community completely dependent on the two-faced charms of a nuclear reactor power plant.

The children watched the shimmering flames, fire trucks and dive-bombing helicopters from the windows of their two-room apartments nearby. Many of their fathers worked at the reactor and were courageously attempting to combat the toxic fires. Some of the children had been told not to open the windows, so they had to look at the fireworks through the steamed-up glass. Soon they were growing restless. They were told to keep their shoes on around the house, which seemed odd. And some of them were given small white tablets. Many parents in Pripyat decided to keep their children away from school on Monday; those children who went were sent home by their teachers. The government had suddenly ordered the people of Pripyat to evacuate immediately. Everyone was bewildered and disoriented. Told to walk five kilometres (3 miles) out of town, they were forbidden to carry anything with them. They left their toys, schoolbooks, clothes and furniture. They didn't know when they would see them again, but they had been reassured they wouldn't be gone for ever. They tried to be brave, despite the frightening circumstances. As they reached the forests outside the town, they saw hundreds of buses revving up. Clouds of choking exhaust fumes were drifting among the trees. Within thirty-six hours of the disaster the entire population had been bussed out and Pripyat became a ghost town. Every household was forced to depart in such a hurry that beds were left unmade, breakfast was still on the table and washing up was piled up in the sink. The evacuated residents were driven to a tented city near Slavutich, 100 kilometres (60 miles) away. They were ordered to strip and were led into flapping canvas tents for decontamination. Their clothing was taken and burned. They were pushed into makeshift army showers. Their roubles were exchanged for new money and the old notes and coins were buried.

In the city of Gomel, 160 kilometres (100 miles) north-east of the reactor, the local Communist Party issued an order that everyone should stay within the confines of their apartment blocks. Then, four days after the disaster, when the pressure of waiting inside had grown to boiling point, the government suddenly claimed the situation was stable. They said the residents of Gomel and other towns nearby were free to go outside to join in the traditional May Day celebrations. There was collective relief at the news.

It had been raining lightly and now a warm sun was filtering through the clouds. The families streamed into the parks and prepared to celebrate with the costumes, banners and flags they had made during the previous weeks. A lot of black goo had fallen on to the ground in the spring rain. It stuck to their shoes, so they wiped it off, unaware that it was contaminated material from the sky. When the parades in the towns and cities cheerfully set off, most people were wearing light summery clothes, grateful to feel the warmth on their skin after days spent cooped up inside. But when the crowds cheerfully marched past the parade stand, where the city leaders and army officials usually sat, they could see only the strangest fancy dress. Every person in the stand was dressed from head to toe in baggy white cotton suits. Fabric helmets like beekeepers' hats were draped over their heads down to their shoulders. Where their faces should have been were smoky glass visors. With a chill, the marching locals realized that these were radiation suits. They looked at the bare, freckled arms of their children and were afraid.

After the explosion, the authorities had pulled out charts and drawn a circle extending thirty kilometres (20 miles) around the reactor. Anyone living inside the 'dead zone' would have to leave. But it is impossible to draw a neat line around a radiation zone, however important the person looking at the map. The deadly cloud was drifting further north across 1,600 kilometres (1,000 miles) of north-western Europe. The nuclear fall-out it was carrying was blown by the wind, settling on the ground and seeping into the nearby water meadows and sand flats. It was gradually being absorbed into the water supply and silently entering the food chain.

Officials sent radiation experts swarming over the countryside to measure the levels with specialized machinery. Sometimes the experts found 'hot spots' – areas of lethally high con-tamination sixty to eighty kilometres (40-50 miles) from the reactor. Where the levels of radiation were found to be off the top of the scale, the maps were marked with purple patches and soon looked like bodies covered in painful bruises. Yet at other times, the men with the Geiger counters found corners of fields within sight of the reactor that didn't even register on the dial, despite the fact that they should have been lethally hot. Radiation was just so unpredictable. It was certainly no respector of boundaries.

Gradually the order came through that the outlying communities would have to be evacuated as well. In the vil-lages near Pripyat, the inhabitants knew something terrible had happened. They had seen buses full of refugees travelling at speed along the main roads. They had seen the ominous black clouds hanging in the sky. But they didn't understand what had happened at the concrete building along the road, a factory which for twelve years had provided them with the miracle of lighting in their simple wooden houses at night.

These were country people. They had lived all their lives on the lush, fertile land, growing their crops of potatoes, cabbages and beans. They hadn't studied science. They didn't under-stand radiation. At first, they refused to obey the order to leave. They could see hills between them and the reactor, and assumed that these were natural shields which would protect them from anything nasty in the next valley. They had no way of grasping the scale and extent of radiation's malignant reach. So some villages were visited by Soviet scientists who explained in simple terms that to stay could be fatal. The vil-lagers' children had grown up on milk from their cows, eggs from their chickens and meat from their pigs. Now they were being told that they should no longer eat these things. They found it impossible to believe that their home-grown produce, which looked so nutritious and healthy, could actually kill them. They couldn't believe that they would have to abandon the homes where their families had lived for generations. They certainly wouldn't leave without their cattle. Only when local government officials promised to bring in high-sided trucks to evacuate their cows out with them did the villagers even consider leaving. They reluctantly agreed when they were promised that the village leaders would ride in the trucks with the animals to make sure no harm came to them.

The evacuations of the 5,000 people in the forbidden zone were painfully slow. There was little that could be done to make the people safe. The small white tablets that some of the children had been given contained stable iodine, an element which is taken up by the thyroid gland, preventing it from absorbing radioactive iodine from the reactor. Most adults were given nothing to counteract the effects.

While the villages were being steadily stripped of human life, the contaminated cloud continued to bleed out across the countryside. So in cities near the reactor another convoy had begun in the weeks after the disaster. In Kiev, 130 kilometres south, half a million children were bussed out of the city and away from Chernobyl's lethal range. They were being sent on enforced holidays, far from the radioactive parks and the contaminated water supply to safe countryside further south. Their tearful parents and all other adults were left behind as the buses swept out, towards safety.

The children looked out of the bus windows at the peculiar sight of giant pieces of soggy carpet lining the streets of their beautiful city. They had been placed there to damp down radiation. Splashes of water sprayed the bus windows from the sprinklers set up to wash their city. The officials had ordered this to be done three times daily. Dousing every pavement and every building up to the level of the first floor was the only way they knew to try to deal with the radioactive dust.

As the buses zoomed out through checkpoints which circled the city, the children could see men in sinister rubber breathing-masks and protective clothing monitoring the cars driving into the town for radioactivity. Any vehicle found to exceed the limit was being turned away.

It felt so strange in Kiev once the thousands of children had left. People had no choice but to try to keep living as normally as possible. They walked in the parks and even fished in the River Dnieper, despite being warned not to. Yet the schools were abandoned and the playgrounds were silent. Lemonade-dispensing machines in the centre of towns were deserted. The ice-cream stalls were shuttered up.

In the parks, babushkas – well-built elderly women wearing traditional white headscarves – were cutting grass to make hay, as they did every year. Although they had been told it was unusable because of the deadly isotopes it now contained and should be buried, it seemed important to keep up with tradition and maintain some normality in the face of such confusion. In the market-places, anxious peasant women displayed their potatoes and onions, but on top of the scrubbed wooden tables were new additions to their stalls – small white certificates neatly initialled by the market director. These showed that the produce on sale had just passed the scrutiny of a radiation test after feverish washing.

In the city hospitals many of the firemen who had fought so courageously against the burning reactor were dying. There was nothing the doctors could do to halt the onslaught of the radiation which was rapidly destroying their bodies. They had only basic medical equipment, which was years out of date, and weren't equipped to handle such a disaster.

Then American multi-millionaire, Dr Armand Hammer, who enjoyed close links with the Soviet Union, had a brainwave. Sitting in his house overlooking the crashing waves of a Californian beach and reading about the nuclear disaster on the other side of the world, he wondered whether bone-marrow transplants might not aid the dying men. The cells that radiation kills first are those that grow fastest – the ones inside the mouth, the stomach and the bones. Because cancerous cells divide the quickest of all this is why controlled doses of radiation are sometimes used to treat cancer. A bone-marrow transplant is an operation where the soft centre of the hipbone from a healthy person is gently sucked out and injected into the bone of the patient. The theory is that the healthy person's bone marrow will increase rapidly, replacing the diseased and radioactive material. It is a little like throwing seeds on newly turned earth: hopefully, some of the healthy cells will take root and the body will again be able to manufacture its own.

Dr Hammer telephoned the world's leading bone-marrow expert, Dr Robert Gale, who lived in Los Angeles, and said he would pay for him to fly a team out to the Soviet Union. In all the years of his career, Dr Gale had been planning for such an emergency, but he had never thought he would come face to face with young men so brutally damaged by other people's carelessness. When Dr Gale arrived at Moscow's Hospital Number Six with bone-marrow supplies from Britain, he found many men who urgently needed a transplant. They were lying silently, barely able to communicate, in solitary rooms. Most of them were only in their twenties. Their bodies had been burned by radioactive dust particles. They had hacking coughs, caused by contaminated smoke particles inhaled into the sensitive lung tissue. The bitter irony was that these men were heroes. All over the Soviet Union, village councils and city leaders were clamouring to rename roads and parks after the firemen who had saved so many lives by their courage.

Dr Gale had spent many years among desperately ill cancer patients, but he felt completely overwhelmed by the scale of the firemen's suffering in the Moscow hospital. He had only a limited amount of bone marrow and just a few weeks to do what he could to help. He faced a difficult decision. Whom should he try to save? It felt uncomfortably like playing God, but he decided that he would operate on the men who had received more than 500 roentgens – the lethal radioactive dose. First he had to conduct tests to see if the men's tissues would accept the bone marrow he had brought with him. If he didn't match the right men with the right samples, their bodies would reject the marrow and the transplant would fail. His crack team of specialists worked fifteen hours a day. Although most of the men who received the precious bone marrow have since died, Dr Gale was able to give them a few more months in which to say goodbye to their wives and children.

The radioactive cloud continued to glide further north. By now it was stealthily smearing contamination from the Soviet Union to Scandinavia and much of northern Europe. The particles were blown higher and higher into the jet stream. The contaminated cloud's deadly cargo was 100 million curies of radiation. It bled across borders carried by wind and water. It blew on to hill farms in North Wales. It rained over the fjords of Norway. It dusted the ice-flats in Lapland where reindeer herds lived. It even interfered with the hazelnut crop in Turkey. Gradually, the radiation seeped into the food chain, growing inside new plants eaten by cattle whose meat then became radioactive.

An area the size of England was eventually so contaminated that it will be unsafe to live in for thousands of years. Although Chernobyl is in the Ukraine, most of the deadly isotopes fell on the neighbouring republic of Belarus. Radiation levels there were 100 times greater than those resulting from the nuclear bombs dropped on the Japanese cities of Hiroshima and Nagasaki at the end of the Second World War.

Gradually, more and more of the evacuated children were becoming sick with eye problems and blood disorders. Many of those who had been evacuated from Pripyat were barely able to stand up a few days later. Their skin had turned a bluish colour and they weren't hungry. When they arrived in the resettlement camps, their future was bleak. They had left behind the newly poisoned rivers, trees and gardens of their childhood and been bussed to a concrete jungle.

The worst was yet to come when the children's radiation

levels were measured. After each reading the children were presented with different coloured labels to wear – not to show where they came from or how old they were, but to signify just how far the Geiger counter needle had shot around the dial. A red label was the worst kind: it meant no one could touch you. Children who had always been popular were suddenly out-casts. Over half the children had received a dangerous dose.

Children who had been forced to abandon their homes in the deadly and deserted countryside met up with children from nearly 2,000 other towns and villages and were rehoused in ugly apartment blocks in the capital city of Minsk, with no furniture, no heating, no soul – like cage after cage of rabbit hutches in an experimental lab. Some of the children had been told they were leaving for only three days, but this was just a way to entice them into the bus convoys. It sometimes took parents months to find their children in the labyrinthine build-ings in the new cities. When they were reunited, families often disintegrated under the strain. Husbands and wives had been forced to leave their lives behind and there was sometimes nothing left to hold them together. Love no longer seemed strong enough in this bleak, alien environment. But those who had been resettled were, in a bizarre sense, the lucky ones. No one had told the other villagers about the invisible dangers. Some were informed but couldn't be moved for years. During this time they lived as usual, eating their contaminated vege-tables, milk, eggs and meat, and becoming steadily sicker with-out understanding why.

Meanwhile, sixty-five kilometres (40 miles) to the north of the Chernobyl reactor and just twenty-five kilometres (15 miles) from the limit of the enforced evacuation zone, the town of Bragin was among the many hundreds in turmoil. During the six months since the disaster, the 17,000 inhabitants knew that everyone inside the exclusion zone had been forcibly relo-cated. They also knew that their town was in the twilight zone: neither officially in the zone nor officially beyond radiation's

23

deadly reach. Or, at least, some people knew that. They were the ones packing up their houses and getting out. They had taken what possessions they could carry on to the backs of their horse-drawn carts or into their ageing Lada cars and gone.

But other people were reluctant to leave, particularly the farmers, and especially if they weren't being forced by the authorities to go. Some stayed, but washed down their houses with foaming buckets of hot water and soap powder just to be on the safe side. One farmer wrapped his prize cow in polythene, believing that this would protect it from radiation. He didn't realize that radioactive nuclides were entering through the animal's mouth. Most of the inhabitants felt grateful that the government hadn't told them to leave the homes they had made, on the land they knew, near their friends. They were sceptical about their neighbours' claims and decided that the radiation rumours sweeping the village were exaggerated.

Natacha and Sergei were one such couple. Both aged twenty-one, they hadn't been married long. Soon after the disaster, they had heard about the evacuations near the power plant but had decided they were far enough away for it to be safe to stay. Their greatest fear was the unknown. Leaving the village where they had met and married would ruin their future, and that felt like a far greater threat to happiness. Radiation sounded like just so much hocus-pocus. Within a few months of the disaster they had virtually forgotten about it. They had far better news. Natacha had been terribly sick for some time and now they knew why. She was pregnant with their first child. Next year she would give birth to a baby. It was a new beginning, a new life.

Chapter 3 The Birth

Natacha's baby was born on 29 March 1987, eleven months after the Chernobyl disaster. Natacha could hear her baby gurgling, but it was the reaction of the staff that concerned her. They weren't saying anything. She craned her head to catch a glimpse of her baby, but the surgeon was blocking her view. He was standing in front of the midwife, who was washing the child at the steel sink. Then he muttered something before turning to Natacha, who was now clutching the white sheets with equally bleached fingers.

'A boy . . . disabled,' said the surgeon.

Fear grabbed at Natacha's heart. How disabled? What did that mean? Oh, she wanted to see him. The midwife dried him and brought him over to her.

Half of her baby's tiny body seemed to be missing. Although his head, covered in downy dark brown hair, was perfectly formed, he appeared to have no legs. His feet were like little flippers, emerging directly from his tiny thighs. On his left foot there were just two miniature toes, on his right foot there were three. Natacha looked for his right arm. There wasn't one. The baby's perfect red face wasn't screwed up ready to cry; instead he was blinking his deep brown eyes at the delivery-room lights. But it was too much to assume that he would be only mildly brain damaged. Natacha did not know how to react, what to do, or who could help her. She wondered if she could cope with a severely disabled child.

She looked at the flippers and the missing arm of her vulnerable baby. She remembered her terrible sickness throughout the pregnancy. She had vomited regularly, even before she had known she was pregnant. She had suffered constant headaches throughout her confinement. She had had little energy and poor skin. But she had assumed these were natural consequences of pregnancy. Now she felt sick and fearful. Did this have something to do with people's warnings about the damaged reactor?

Chernobyl was just sixty-five kilometres (40 miles) south of her home. Three months or so after the disaster she had realized she was expecting a child, but no one had warned her about the dangers of becoming pregnant. She had heard some talk of women from the contaminated area being advised to terminate their pregnancies, but she hadn't understood why or thought it would apply to her. Anyway, she lived so far from the site of the reactor. She had never even seen it. The threats about radiation certainly hadn't seemed to apply to her, so she had never considered the dreadful possibility that the disaster might have an impact on her unborn child. After all, he had been safely protected within her.

Now she could feel the painful fingers of guilt prodding her. She and her husband both had to work to afford the rent on their two-room apartment. Such a child as this would require constant nursing and care. What's more, would anyone talk to her if she had such a child? Would she be labelled an outcast for producing a disabled baby? Would he be rejected? Natacha knew great sympathy was given to parents who felt unable to cope with a brain-damaged baby.

She looked at the midwife holding the incomplete child, whose body bore the damaging legacy of radiation. Without touching him, she forced herself to say, 'I don't want him.' Neither did she want to touch him; she knew that would make it difficult ever to let go. Instead, she rolled away from the quiet child and fixed her eyes at the peeling plaster on the wall. The bed was hard. Inside she was screaming, but externally she tried to stay calm. She would put this behind her. She would put the flawed baby out of her head. She comforted herself with the fact that he would be well cared for. And he wouldn't be aware of the world anyway, for, his mother believed, he had no mind with which to miss her. She would have another child later on, when the radiation levels had dropped. Maybe she and Sergei would move away from Bragin and start again.

Little is known about Igor's parents. A Belarussian law allows a couple to abandon a disabled child with the minimum of difficulty and this was their decision. Sergei came to collect Natacha and in stunned silence they signed their new baby over to the state. Then they walked away from the hospital, childless, despairing that Natacha had inhaled great lungfuls of radiation and eaten contaminated food without understanding the deadly power of the nuclear disaster.

Before she left the hospital, Natacha named her baby Igor. What she and Sergei didn't know was that Igor's brain wasn't damaged. In fact, he was extremely bright.

Once his parents had signed him over to the authorities at the hospital, Igor had no one. Today, his parents may be dead, they may be alive – no one knows. The nurses swaddled the new baby tightly in white towelling. Carefully bound in the traditional manner with many layers of cloth, he looked like a little sausage roll with a sweet face peering out of the pastry. Igor stayed in the maternity home for eleven days while his papers were prepared and he was legally separated from his family.

For the first eleven months of his life he was shuttled from one hospital in Minsk to another, but nothing could be done for his deformities, so after a short time at Hospital Number Two, he was taken to the equally imaginatively named Children's Home Number One, one of thirteen homes for young children in Minsk, where sixty-five abandoned boys and girls lived in seven dormitories.

The driver pulled up outside the three-storey building painted in flaking red, yellow and green, and a nurse carried the baby no one wanted up the flights of concrete steps. Once inside, the nurse walked briskly to Dr Ludmilla Kravchenko's office. She was the chief doctor and could sign yet more paperwork.

The nurse rapped on the door. Ludmilla's gaze was immediately drawn to the appealing bundle which the nurse was holding. He was beautiful. His dark brown eyes shone. She quickly signed the papers and sat the baby on her lap. Gently, she examined him. Instinctively, he wrapped his left arm around her neck and nuzzled her. She saw his stunted legs and felt for his right arm, finding instead the small mound. A feeling of dread washed over her. Medical training had taught her to fear radiation. Here, calmly cradled on her lap, was a little boy who was evidence of the radiation which had seeped everywhere. She felt a cold chill and hugged the baby tighter to her chest, rocking him gently back and forth and murmuring to him. It was just as she had feared. During the months after the meltdown she had thought of all the pregnant women and wondered what it was doing to their unborn children.

She wondered now if the baby's mother would ever come to visit. Women who gave birth to deformed children often abandoned them but would sometimes journey to the children's home in the hope that between visits their child had improved. Loudmila feared that, with the extent of Igor's deformities, this would be unlikely.

She took Igor along the corridor, up staircases painted with gold stars and along to one of the wards painted in a soft sunflower yellow. She placed him in a cot by a vast window. She pulled white cotton curtains printed with bright yellow flowers across to shield him from the sunlight. She despaired at the enormous windows which made the building inadequate for its purpose: in summer it was always blistering hot, in winter it was always freezing. Ludmilla arranged for Igor to be christened, something she did for every child who arrived in the hospital. If his natural parents couldn't care for him, God would. Despite the fact that the Communist Party had officially suppressed religion, people's faith continued.

Igor's cot was in a row in the centre of the dormitory. It had thin metal bars through which he could peer out at the lines of other cots and playpens. The dormitory was to be the only home he would have for the next six years. There was to be no Mummy or Daddy, no brothers or sisters; just kindly female nurses and mentally and physically handicapped children. Cuddles would always be shared. Privacy would be impossible. His whole life would be acted out in the centre of the dormitory, under the bright lights and the scrutiny of the scurrying nurses, who worked twenty-four hours at a stretch and then had three days off.

Igor was a very smiley, happy baby. The nurses immediately realized that his mind was developing normally. His problems were all physical and this made him unique among the other children. He was not brain-damaged in any way and was responsive and interested in everything. His cheerful nature made him the darling of the nurses, especially Lilya Greenhouse. She had a grey perm, smiling grey eyes and narrow lips. Traditionally, people with thin lips are considered cruel and ruthless, but Lilya was the opposite: very kind and gentle.

She was immediately drawn to the small child. Sometimes after lunch the nurses would set records spinning on a record player in the ward. It was one of the few ways they had to stimulate the children, hoping the gaiety of the music would provoke and excite them. Igor loved music. He was captivated by the feelings it created in his body and couldn't resist the urge to start moving. He would call out for Lilya, grabbing her hand, and she would scoop him up and dance with him, shuffling around in her low-heeled shoes and thick tights as the baby giggled with delight.

During the day, Lilya picked up Igor as often as she could. If he wasn't carried, he could only watch the other children playing from his bed. He didn't learn to toddle at the usual time because of his deformities. Lilya would chatter to Igor about everything in the ward and outside in the garden. She would

29

name objects, hoping that it might make up for life in an institution a little, and help him to develop as normally as possible.

She would sit him down in the play area and give him a toy car. Sometimes she would slip a new one out of her battered leather handbag. His eyes would shine and he would try to find out what was inside the cars. He would investigate to see if any parts opened or lifted up or disconnected. Then, when he had satisfied his inquisitive mind, he would push them hard so they sped away across the floor. Inevitably, Igor was possessive of Lilya. As far as he was concerned, Lilya was his special nurse, so when she took another child out for a walk in the garden, Igor was jealous and felt angry. He would stare intently at the toy car he was playing with and concentrate all his attention on it, until Lilya came back into the ward. Then, forgetting his anger, he would call out for her. The rest of the time he was a generous child. When she brought him presents of sweets and biscuits, he would always give one to each child in the group.

Every day rolled past with the same regime, even Saturdays and Sundays. The children would be woken up at quarter to seven in the morning. The other children were dressed by the nurses, but Igor always tried to put on his own clothes. He would wear woolly tights and colourful jumpers. At eight o'clock those who were old enough would sit at small blue-Formica-topped tables for breakfast. Wearing bibs, they would scoop up porridge, rice pudding or semolina. They would sip weak tea and eat a piece of bread and butter. The babies would be fed on powdered milk made up with water. After breakfast the children would sit outside in the garden, play in yellow playpens with black rubber foam bases or be taught to draw with coloured pencils if they were able to hold them. Lunch was soup with boiled rice, pasta or mashed potatoes. Sometimes there was chicken or beef floating in the watery broth. After lunch the children would be put down to sleep for two hours. When they awoke, after taking their coats from their lockers, they could go for a walk or a pram-ride in the garden if the weather was fine. Igor was very independent and since he always liked to dress himself, his locker was closest to the dormitory. Each locker had a different hand-painted symbol stuck to its door. The children liked to pull these off and swap them around, so sometimes Igor's locker symbol was a strawberry, at other times a cherry or a flower.

If it was raining, the children would spend the afternoon inside, playing with the nurses if they had time. There was a talking parrot in a cage and goldfish in an aquarium. Igor was fascinated by everything. At four o'clock the children would be given a snack of biscuits washed down with a cup of milk or orange juice. They would have a sleep before the evening meal of porridge, semolina, rice pudding and vegetables. Then the lights were switched out at eight o'clock and there was supposed to be total hush.

Igor was usually a very obedient little boy, but when he heard Lilya tiptoeing into the ward on the evening shift after the lights had been turned off, he was unable to resist the urge to shout out her name. He knew that she would come over to hold him and he loved to be cuddled. Each time he called to her, the other children would wake in their cots and start shouting out as well. Lilya would sigh, smile, take off her woollen coat and hang it on the brass peg, before creeping into the ward. She would softly calm the other children down, stroking their faces and murmuring soothing words to them. Then she would walk towards Igor, sitting upright in his cot, a huge smile on his face and his eyes shining at her. As she reached him, he would stretch out his hand and catch hold of her white overalls. Lilya would cradle him, singing the Russian lullabies she had learned as a child, and Igor would then fall asleep, blissfully content.

Ludmilla also loved to cuddle Igor. She felt frustrated that there was so little she could do for him. She knew that if he had been born in the West, there would have been so many treatments the surgeons could have attempted to improve his quality of life and his legs could have been operated on to turn his little feet forward. But she knew these were just dreams. Nothing like this was possible in Belarus, where a packet of aspirins cost the equivalent of half a month's salary.

More and more damaged babies had begun arriving. Some of them seemed all right on first sight, but they would turn out to have sealed ears, or thumbs which branched into two fingertips, each with a perfect nail. Before the Chernobyl disaster, the dormitories had been filled mainly with children whose mothers had abandoned them because they were unmarried or too poor to raise them. There had always been some physically and mentally handicapped children, but in the months after the nuclear disaster the number of flawed children who were being born and abandoned had more than trebled. Some of the nurses had worked there for over thirty years and they were astounded by the sudden increase in deformities. Gradually the dormitories were filling up with profoundly damaged babies and children. Many of them had defects caused by the radioactive food eaten by their mothers. Nobody wanted them and they were destined to spend the rest of their lives in institutions, as a hidden but very persuasive reminder of the Chernobyl disaster.

In February 1989, Children's Home Number One was officially turned into a specialist centre for physically deformed children. This meant that, like twelve other children's homes, it now fell under the jurisdiction of the Ministry of Health, which had discovered that disorders of the central nervous system and developmental defects were increasing every year. Children were at maximum risk if they had been exposed to radiation in the womb.

Two months later, Ludmilla left and was replaced by Dr Tamara Mourashova. Tamara was a delicate-looking blonde woman of thirty-one with deep blue eyes. She too was immediately charmed by Igor. Because his legs were missing, he seemed so tiny, but it was his face which surprised her. He had such an intelligent gaze. Instantly, she felt great love, compassion and pity for the child.

Deformed children continued to arrive at the hospital. One day a baby whose head was three times too big was delivered, his eyes bulging under the pressure from his brain. He softly moaned, but Tamara knew he was unaware of who or where he was. One child who arrived had no arms, another no ears. One child's legs were so badly bent and twisted that they looked like a coat hanger. Another had a severe hair lip and cleft palate – a crater which opened up the centre of his face. This defect, easily corrected in the rest of Europe, could not be dealt with here. Such children would go through life with a hole in their face, never learning to talk and always facing rejection. There were Down's Syndrome babies, rocking back and forward obsessively. And an infant with severe spina bifida, who had a lump the size of an adult fist on his back. It was becoming a children's hospital rather than a children's home.

Tamara wondered how she could ever help them all. The government had run out of money and stopped buying new equipment and medicines. She wasn't able to sedate children who were in pain because of their illnesses. It was difficult even to sustain life, let alone help. As more and more deformed children arrived, Tamara began to see the effect they were having on her young unmarried nurses. They had become fearful of their own chances of conceiving a healthy baby. One by one, the nurses left. Tamara replaced them with matronly women like Lilya, who were too old to have children, or whose sons and daughters had already left home.

Igor wasn't concerned by the shocking deformities of these other children and was very gentle with them. All the children in the children's home loved to be hugged by adults. Because Igor was developing normally mentally and could show affection, the other children clung to him as if he were an adult. He was so used to seeing other children with greater physical and mental problems, he never appeared to feel despair or helplessness at his own situation.

Sometimes Lilya would bring Igor books with pictures of cars in them. He would concentrate intently and pick out the ones he wanted to drive when he was older. At the moment, he could barely move around his cot by himself and he so longed to walk. When he was sitting on the floor, playing with the other children, he would look at their shoes. Perhaps that was the problem, he wondered, maybe his shoes were wrong. He went through a phase of undoing his leather buckles, kicking off his shoes and leaning over to the other children to pull off theirs. They weren't able to complain as Igor tried to fit his feet inside in his desperate attempt to discover the secret of walking.

Chapter 4 The Garden

When Igor was two years old, Lilya decided it was time to teach him to walk. There were few nurses and many children in the dormitories, so if the other nurses were busy, they would leave the children in their cots most of the day. But Lilya had often taken Igor into the grassy garden at the back of the children's home. She had wanted him to spend lots of time outside in the fresh air, because she could see he was unusually talented and alert. It just seemed to make sense that bright sunshine would help him.

Each afternoon that Lilya was working at the children's home in the spring of 1989, she would settle herself on the grass outside while Igor tried to stand upright by himself, steadying himself against her broad back. His feet were turned out sideways, so balancing was difficult. He had never seen anyone else with a body like his, so he had no one else to copy and had to work out his own methods for standing and walking. Because his arm touched the ground, Lilya told him to lean on it. For weeks, she would patiently encourage him to use it like a third leg. Igor loved the attention she was paying him. Lilya would always reward him with a hug, so he tried as hard as he could with absolute determination. He would tell every nurse and visitor to the hospital, 'Lilya is teaching me to walk.' He glowed with pride and practised constantly. His speech had also advanced a little. Speech usually comes at the same time as the ability to walk but because Igor had always been surrounded with children too handicapped to talk, he hadn't been immersed in normal happy chatter. When he spoke he did so very slowly. Tamara was concerned by the way he seemed to be lagging behind normal children in his development.

When he was two and a half, Igor could finally walk and run. He would race up and down the ward, swinging his arm on to the ground like a chimpanzee to propel his legs forward. From that point on, when he saw Lilya or one of the other nurses pulling out the record player and selecting a record, he would race on to the empty linoleum floor and await the exciting crackling sound just before the first notes. As he got older, he would excitedly turn cartwheels and spin around on one hand when the Russian folk music began. The nurses would gently coax the other children to join in.

Because all the nurses were female, Igor had seen few men and they were a novelty. A male driver, Misha, sometimes worked at the children's home, bringing food and driving the doctors to appointments. Igor became very friendly with Misha, partly because he was a man and partly because he was a driver and Igor loved cars. Misha was a source of fascination to all the boys in the children's home, but he took a particular shine to Igor and would sit him down on the passenger seat and let him toot the horn. Igor's fascination with cars grew stronger by the day. He yearned to have a car of his own and seemed almost hypnotized by the thought of the mobility it could provide.

Now he could walk, Lilya was able to push back the horizons of Igor's world a little further. Rather than staying in the confines of the children's home, they would walk up quiet streets shaded by avenues of trees in the south-western suburbs of Minsk. Sometimes Igor would experience the ultimate thrill: a ride on a trolley bus. He was fascinated by the speed at which he was moving. He loved pressing the bell to make the bus slow down, clambering off and watching the bus rumble off without him. Then he would stand on the pavement, watching the cars charge past. 'Buy me that car, Lilya,' he would demand, pointing at the spluttering Ladas, the most

36

popular car in Belarus. These weren't sleek, impressive cars, but rather grumpy tin cans. To Igor, they were the most exciting things he had ever seen.

Shortly after his third birthday, Igor's kind, sweet nature appeared to be changing. He gradually became more aggressive. He would throw his toys around and push the other children. Fortunately, the nurses immediately made a connection: Igor had started looking in the mirror. He was comparing his body with those of the other children and he'd seen that he was different. To their great credit, the nurses immediately began to confront the problem. They told him over and over again that his deformities didn't make him different. They also told him that they believed that one day he would be helped and be given new limbs to make him look like other children.

On the 12 April 1990, Tamara phoned a research institute in Moscow to apply for artificial limbs for Igor. It looked hopeful, so Igor travelled 500 kilometres (300 miles) by train to meet the consultant. But the moment the specialist saw the extent of Igor's deformities, he shook his head. There wasn't the expertise to help him and Igor was forced to return to the children's home in Minsk. The nurses tried to explain the specialist's reasons, but Igor was wounded by the refusal. Tamara felt guilty that she had given him such hope, so she started taking Igor home to play with her two boys. She also made inquiries at Children's Home Number Three, to see if Igor could be transferred. The children there suffered only slight learning difficulties and Igor would have the benefit of some schooling. She urgently wanted him to mix with normal children, because his ability to structure sentences was weak, but he was refused admission because of the extent of his deformities. The nurses there didn't think they had the time to cope with such a physically deformed child. They focused on petty issues. 'Such a child would get wet when walking in the rain because his lower body is so close to the pavement,' they said. Tamara responded by customizing Igor a pair of waterproof trousers cut from one of her son's wet-weather gear. She could see only practical solutions, but she soon realized that Children's Home Number Three didn't want Igor. This bright little chap didn't fit in anywhere: he was too intelligent for Children's Home Number One, too deformed for Number Three.

Igor had a dream that had begun to consume him. He shuttled around the lino floor, propelling himself with his strong arm and roaring with laughter, but he had begun to think constantly about the independence a right arm would give him. Sometimes he went to sleep thinking that if he wished hard enough, one would start to grow. He would touch his shoulder and ask, 'Why haven't I got an arm here?' The nurses would explain that it just hadn't grown. There was another little boy in the ward without hands and both Igor and he were encouraged not to lose hope but to believe that one day a man would come who could help them. Igor seized hold of this thought. Every time an unfamiliar man visited the children's home, he would become very excited. He would catch the man by the trousers and demand, 'Give me an arm and give me legs.' He would bombard the nurses with the same question every day: 'When is the man coming who can help me?' All they could say was 'one day soon'. Igor wasn't told why he had no right arm. The nurses didn't mention Chernobyl because they didn't think the children would understand but other than his powerful desire for an arm, Igor's life felt like normality and he assumed this was how all children lived. He had never heard the words Mummy and Daddy, so he had nothing to miss.

Lilya had been married twice, but had never had children and Igor had become the sunlight of her life. Her next challenge was teaching him to read. She didn't know what his future held and there was every chance it could be very bleak, but she wanted to equip him to cope in the outside world should he be lucky enough ever to meet it. She found some flashcards with words printed on them. Gradually Igor learned to recognize a few letters and to draw them slowly on pieces of paper.

His future was bleak because Children's Home Number One could not be his home for ever. The rules said that at four years of age the handicapped children must move on to an adult institution – and rules in the Soviet Union mattered terribly. It was hard enough to see the mentally handicapped children being taken off to a place where few people would have the time or inclination to cuddle and play with them. Tamara found it utterly inconceivable that the authorities wanted this to be the fate of children whose only misfortune was to have been born deformed and left alone.

The adult mental institutions were located the other side of town. The children's wing was a two-storey concrete building which smelt of musty apples. Some of the windowpanes were broken and paint was flaking off the ceilings and walls. Far worse was the noise. The children inside, distressed and unloved, moaned often. Children of six and seven banged their heads against the flimsy bars in a repetitive rocking action. Staff busied themselves with ministering to the children's needs: changing sheets, feeding them soup, cleaning them up. There was no time for the staff to cuddle and soothe these fragile children, however much they might have wanted to. The impoverished government had no money to invest in making such institutions happier.

Tamara thought of Igor, who was still too young to go to the institution, and worried terribly about his future. In such an environment as this there was no way that such an intelligent and loving little boy as he would be able to thrive and develop. Of course, Igor knew nothing about the dark threats that hung over his future. Everything in his world was contained in the warm dormitory with Tamara, the nurses and of course, Lilya. Tamara picked up Igor and cuddled him. Her modest salary – the equivalent of £35 a month for seventy hours' work a week – was once again overdue and she had no food in the fridge at home, but she didn't want to let Igor go. Her purse might be empty and she knew that in any other job she could walk out in protest at not being paid, but not here. She couldn't possibly abandon these children, not when she and the nurses under her instruction were all they had, even if it meant her own children and her husband, a computer programmer, had to go without certain things. She was working thirteen hours a day, six days a week. She simply didn't have time to complain.

One Wednesday afternoon, Lilya decided to sit down during the dancing session. Igor ran over to her. 'Lilya, dance with me,' he implored. 'I can't do this,' she said. 'I'm just a tired, grey-haired old granny.' Igor shook his head. 'You're not a granny. You are Lilya. My Lilya,' and he grabbed her hand, pulled out into the centre of the room and clung to her legs. He was only as tall as the hem on her skirt. His eyes were on a level with her knees, and how he loved to watch Lilya's knees dancing.

Then one day Lilya didn't come to the children's home when she was supposed to. Igor waited by the door for her cheerful, smiling face all afternoon. He did the same the next day, growing ever more anxious. He missed her chunky hugs and sweet-smelling skin. Finally, one of the nurses noticed his sad expression. She sat him on her lap and said, 'Lilya is ill. She's had a heart attack. Her heart is feeling better now, but she won't be able to see you while she rests.' Igor felt very sad. He didn't want to play with his cars that afternoon.

Four months later, Igor was having lunch at the little table. He had a special treat of sausages on his plate. They were skating about as he tried to stab them with his fork and he wished he had another hand to help. Then he heard slow footsteps in the corridor outside and looked round. The other children didn't recognize the grey-haired lady in a woollen coat opening the door into the room, but Igor did. He shrieked, 'Lilya,' slid off his chair and raced across to see her, his face brimming with excitement. They hugged like mother and son.

Lilya wasn't well enough to work at the children's home after her heart attack, but she came to visit Igor whenever she could. She would always come to the children's birthday parties. All the children with a birthday during one particular month would celebrate them together on the same day. They would dress in their best clothes, there would be poetry readings and some of the children would sing. Igor's early years were passing in a blur because one day blended into the next, but the birthday parties were memorable highlights. It was possible to look back and see a day with a difference.

Christmas was not celebrated in the former Soviet Union. Instead, New Year was the most special time of year. The nurses would prop a small pine tree in a bucket and cover it with a set of twinkling lights. Igor was mesmerized. To see a tree inside was such a treat. Then, dressed in his best clothes, donated to the hospitals by German charities, he would await Father Frost, who, he hoped, would bring him a car all of his own. Unfortunately, the cars were only big enough to fit in his pocket, not to get inside.

When Igor was five, one of the younger nurses decided he needed a treat. He was such an intelligent little boy and craved new sensations, so she decided he should be introduced to the outside world. One Sunday she took him to her home in one of Minsk's micro-districts. These soulless suburbs housed the 50,000 resettlers from the contaminated villages, as well as many of the people who were born in Minsk. Nine-storey concrete rabbit hutches stretched in all directions. There were only small patches of grass, trampled by children.

After the trolley bus had dropped them, Igor held the nurse's hand and walked to the high-rise where her two-room apartment was located. The lift wasn't working, so he hopped up the flights of broken-tile stairs on his strong arm, swinging his legs up behind him. There were no light bulbs in the corridors – they had all been stolen – so Igor had to slide his feet carefully along to make sure he didn't fall.

41

His nurse's two-bedroom flat was another world. On the carpeted floor were amazing cushioned seats which felt like they were hugging you when you sat in them. He hopped out of the armchair and loped to the window. Standing on another chair, he could see children playing on slides and swings down below. On the walls of the apartment was shiny flowered paper. To Igor it all seemed so plush and comfortable. And the food served for Sunday lunch was so colourful. He stared at the parsley and fish heads in a clear jelly and the boiled carrot, garnished with a tomato flower. There was even a pile of something which was oozing bright purple paint; he had never seen steamed beetroot before.

Igor was now nearly two years older than the accepted minimum age for the children's home. Tamara was despairing of ever finding a place for him. Since Igor's fourth birthday, she had been telling the authorities that the tiny boy couldn't possibly be more than four. She knew she was stretching the rules, but surely such cruel and restrictive rules were made to be stretched. Life in an institution would not be life at all for an alert and intelligent little boy like Igor. There was also a danger that he might be hurt by the other patients, because his size made him vulnerable.

Tamara knew it was imperative that she did all she could to protect the future of the little boy with the sunny disposition who had the ability to brighten the lives of everyone he met. Sometimes she lay awake at night, dreading the day the men with clipboards would find her special little boy and take him away. They seemed to be so unmoved by the children whom she loved. Igor was growing up. She couldn't wait for ever. But what could she do?

Chapter 5 The Lifeline

Some 1,600 kilometres (1,000 miles) away, in the south of England, a fuzzy-haired retired businessman was going for an early morning walk through his dewy fields. It was late September 1992 and Victor Mizzi's only thoughts were of his unofficial zoo. At the last count he had ten goats, five geese, half a dozen ducks, at least thirty chickens – all competing with each other for the title of Best Egg Layer – and thirty-five sheep with varied wool haircuts. He counted out the morning's offering of thirty-five warm freckled eggs and strode back up the hill towards his fifteenth-century house in the stockbroker belt near Haslemere, Surrey. He heard his Swedish wife, Birgitta, shout out that coffee was ready. Victor, who was in his late fifties, had never planned to take in other people's unwanted farmyard animals. When he had sold his Maltese travel company and taken early retirement in 1985, he had intended to keep only two sheep for grass-chomping duty. But he had soon found he couldn't resist helping unwanted strays, be they feathered or furry.

He had also realized that he needed a project to keep his active mind satisfied. So an advert in the local newspaper three months earlier had really caught his interest. Two local women had been looking for families to give children from the area around the Chernobyl nuclear reactor a holiday. Victor, like most people, had forgotten about the disaster – it had happened over six years ago. But when he heard that there were children who still needed help, he had immediately telephoned and said that he and Birgitta would like to look after two of them. He had then read everything he could find about the

43

plight of the children. Evacuated from their homes in the con-taminated zone, he'd learned, they were still living on radio-active food and developing cancers that couldn't be cured. Most of them were from a small republic called Belarus, which used to be part of the Soviet Union before it broke away and gained independence in 1990. Although Belarus was the most heavily contaminated area, the government there was very poor and couldn't do anything for the sick children.

Something inside Victor had clicked: he couldn't put the children out of his head. Then he'd received a phone call a fortnight before the children were due to arrive to say that their visit had been cancelled because no airline was prepared to help with free flights. Victor had zoomed into action and immediately contacted all the local people who'd wanted to host the children. Within days, he'd formed a committee. Then he'd written to every house in Haslemere, pleading for help. Two weeks later he'd raised £10,500 and his charity Chernobyl Children Life Line had been born.

Victor put the eggs in the fridge and sat in the kitchen with his mug of steaming coffee, opening his mail. There were many letters from people wanting to know how they could become host parents to the Belarussian children on their next visit. The first month-long trip had been a great success. Twenty children had visited and by the time they returned home they were noticeably healthier, with glowing red cheeks, vast arrays of new fillings and clutching bulging holdalls stuffed with baseball caps, trainers, T-shirts, tapes and bubble-gum – presents from their host families.

Among the mail was a large brown envelope with a German postmark, containing an article from a German newspaper. Victor smoothed out its crumpled folds and caught his breath. On the page was a black-and-white photograph of a tiny, nude child, a child from Belarus. A nurse was standing behind him about to shroud him in a towel. The child was deformed in a way Victor had never seen before. He had no right arm and only small, turned-out feet. The article said that the cause of his deformities was the dose of radiation he had received while in his mother's womb. But it was the child's face which stopped Victor in his tracks. He seemed to be staring directly out at him, with a look of such vulnerability and helplessness. The child in the photograph was Igor.

Victor left his coffee untouched on the table and rushed to the phone. He called Maria Obrasova in Belarus. Maria was part of the Belarus charity the 26th April Foundation, which was helping to arrange the older children's visits to Britain. This time Victor had an unusual request for Maria. Could she try to locate a particular boy with no legs and only one arm?

Victor thought the chances of finding the boy were slim, as there must be so many hospitals all over the country. While he waited, he continued to arrange the monthly visits for children of between nine and sixteen to come to Britain. Just a month breathing fresh air and eating uncontaminated food was able to boost their immune system and make them healthier. But Victor couldn't forget Igor's face. Six months later, Maria rang. A Belarus newspaper had just started publishing articles about the impact of the disaster on the new generation of children. With their help she had located the boy. Victor immediately booked a flight.

Flying in low towards the airport in Minsk, Victor looked out of the window at the Belarussian landscape beneath him. To him, the land looked ravaged and dead. Great bruises seemed to discolour the fields, which were completely barren. Much of the land seemed undeveloped, with the remains of pine forests straggling over the desolate plains. The earth here looked as if it could not sustain life.

The airport felt like a tomb. Every surface was covered in slabs of cold grey marble which was chipped at the edges. Men in green uniforms, armed with Kalashnikov rifles, barked into walkie-talkies. They wore flat hats that looked like pancakes. After taking his case from the wonky, creaking luggage carousel, every item of worth in Victor's luggage was logged by three men, who slowly picked through his possessions.

Outside, the women watching for passengers wore bright fuchsia lipstick and had bouffant, brittle hairdos. Everyone's clothes seemed dated and unfashionable, as if they were stuck in a 1950s time-warp. Maria rushed forward to greet Victor. They drove directly to the children's home, along the deserted, main road surrounded by stands of pine trees. There were hardly any cars – few people had the money to afford them. Horses pulling wooden carts laden with straw occasionally clattered past.

In the children's home, Victor was introduced to Tamara Mourashova, who led him slowly through each dormitory. Everything was spotlessly clean, but wherever he looked there were cots filled with sick and deformed children. Tamara led him up the final flight of stairs to the dormitory which was home to the most deformed children. At the far end was a blue table, around which four children were shovelling up vegetable soup and hunks of dried bread as part of their lunch.

Igor wasn't enjoying his lunch very much, so he was delighted when he heard Tamara's voice mingling with a man's. He looked around and stared intently at the visitor. He took in Victor's fuzzy black hair and glasses, and with a big smile immediately gestured for him to come and join him. He pulled off a piece of bread and gave it to the startled man. After all, Igor thought, this could be the one he had been waiting for, the man who would get him an arm and legs. Victor popped his camera on the table. Igor was fascinated, picked it up and wanted to see how every button worked. His record for destroying visitors' cameras was legendary among the nurses.

Victor could sense Igor's intelligence and felt the way his personality seemed to fill the room, obscuring his deformities. He took a photo of him wearing blue dungarees which were rolled up because his legs were so short. In his arms, Igor clutched the pink and yellow teddy bear Victor had given him. The clock was ticking round and the nurses wanted Igor to go to his cot for a sleep, but he couldn't stop smiling and waving at the man.

Tamara told Victor how little money she had to help the children. Victor made no promises to the hospital, but when he arrived home he contacted the *Daily Express* newspaper. The executive editor, Alan Frame, was a kindly man with a luxurious white beard. He had also visited the area near the reactor, but in the Ukraine rather than Belarus, to write articles for the newspaper and he promised to help Victor raise some money. I was sent to meet Victor and write an article about what he had seen in the children's homes and cancer hospitals. The article was headlined 'The Inheritors of Chernobyl' and when it was published, in April 1993, hundreds of letters started flooding in for the charity. They contained a total of £18,000 in donations to buy medicines and to fund more visits to Britain for the older children. Companies also donated palettes of toys and clothes. One letter in particular stood out. It was written by a retired army officer called Vic Tucker. Vic was normally in control of his emotions, but the photograph had constantly nagged his conscience. He felt such sympathy for the lost little boy with the lovely face and found himself writing to Victor Mizzi.

Dear Sir

I write in connection with the harrowing article in the 7 April issue of the *Daily Express*. In particular I was very moved at the plight of the young boy Igor, whose photograph appeared in the article.

I do contribute to various charities and with limited resources it is difficult to do more. I would, however, like to send a parcel which I would make up specifically to Igor.

I would of course be prepared to pay the cost of transportation. Although I am sure your organization helps many like Igor, I do want my contribution to be specific in this instance. I will be out of the UK for about two weeks but I

47

would be delighted to find a favourable reply from you on my return.

Victor immediately wrote back:

Dear Mr Tucker
If you send a small parcel for Igor to me I shall make sure that it will reach him at the children's home. We have parcels going to Belarus with each group that return after their visit to the UK, so it will not be a problem.

Two weeks later a brown-paper parcel the size of two shoe-boxes, tied with string, arrived with the words 'For Igor' written on the crinkled paper. Victor dispatched it with the next group of children returning home. He asked Valentina Chakhlai, his coordinator in Belarus, who was also an academic at the university in Minsk, to take some photographs of Igor opening the present so Vic Tucker could see that the right child had received his gift.

Igor was amazed by the size of the box Tamara was handing him and telling him to open. He excitedly tore off the wrapping, after she had cut the string, and looked inside. A huge red fire engine almost as big as he was! He was six years old and it was the biggest present he had ever received. It had extending ladders, six chunky black wheels, a compartment for the hose and doors which opened. It was the most amazing toy he had ever seen. When Valentina asked him to pose for a photograph, he held it proudly to his chest. In his mind he was no longer Igor Pavlovets, resident of Children's Home Number One. He was a fireman.

Igor and his fire engine were immediately inseparable. He began to dream of driving a real engine when he was older, racing along with siren blazing and blue light flashing. At night he put the toy on a shelf above his bed. Every morning he examined it minutely, before spending hours zooming around

the floor of the dormitory, dousing imaginary blazes and res-
cuing people. There was only one problem: if he was going to
be a real fireman with a helmet and fireproof overalls, he would
need another arm. He started wishing harder, touching his
shoulder every so often to see if it was growing.

But the fire engine was not his only distraction. He also fell
in love. One of the nurses had a four-year-old daughter with
long fair hair. Igor loved to take a comb and gently brush her
flaxen locks, then curl his finger in its length. He had also
turned into Tamara's impish informant. He was always waiting for her when she came to work. He would tell her which
nurses had been smoking, who was late, who went shopping.

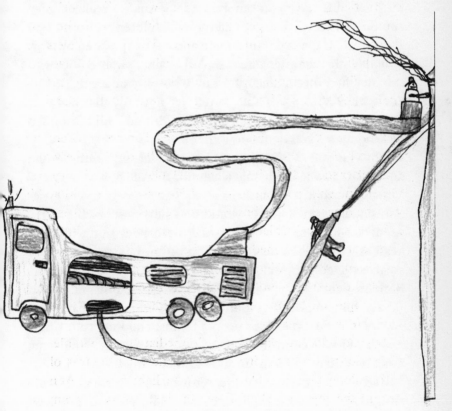

One of many drawings in which Igor draws himself as a heroic firefighter

He wasn't being malicious; he just loved Tamara so much that he wanted to tell her everything.

Vic Tucker was delighted with the photographs. He phoned Victor Mizzi and said he wanted to do more. Before his retirement, he explained, he'd worked as a limb designer at a bionic limb company called Hugh Steeper Ltd, based at Queen Mary's Hospital in Roehampton, south London. He had contacted Steeper's and they were prepared to give Igor a bionic arm for free. For the first time, Victor was able to contact Tamara at the children's home in Minsk to say he could help Igor. He had been hesitant to promise anything before. Two years earlier, a German charity had thought they could help the boy but, having taken him to Germany, realized they couldn't. An Irish charity, Chernobyl Children's Project, had also filmed in the children's home and been captivated by Igor. One day, the charity's director, Adi Roche, phoned Victor to say they had met a delightful boy with only one arm, did he know him? Victor was able to tell her not only that he knew Igor but also that Igor was coming to Britain. Adi responded by sending a £500 donation to help.

The plan was to bring Igor to England for six months for the design and fitting of the magical limb. But the boy would need somewhere to live. Victor was looking for someone very experienced, as caring for Igor would be a huge responsibility. He needed to find someone who could make a decision with their head as well as their heart. He didn't want Igor to end up like an abandoned puppy after Christmas. The obvious choice was Barbara Bennett. Victor knew she was very gentle and would see the boy, not his deformities. Victor had met Barbara after she too had advertised for people to host children from Chernobyl. He had contacted her to say he was doing the same thing, and they had joined forces and become friends.

Barbara had been a foster carer for nearly thirty years. She and her husband, Roy, have five children and fourteen grandchildren of their own, and have fostered about a hundred children, including their foster daughter Sarah, who arrived when she was ten months old for a six-week stay which lasted sixteen years. There have always been at least two children staying at any one time at their house in Farncombe, Surrey. If you count short stays and holiday-placement schemes, over 250 children had been able to call the Bennetts' house home.

Victor's request was a big decision for Barbara. She had never fostered a child as disabled as Igor. Would he be able to adapt to her busy regime? She was also a registered childminder, so the house was always overflowing with demanding pre-schoolers aged from six months to five years during school hours, and older children afterwards. She also knew it would be vital for Igor to feel comfortable with her. She needed to meet him.

When she flew with Victor to Minsk one weekend in October 1993, Barbara still felt totally unsure. They were welcomed with the traditional Slavonic greeting outside the airport terminal in the chilly winter air: a plate of salt and a loaf of bread. Salt used to be very expensive and bread was the staple food, so this was a symbolic sharing of the two most precious commodities.

They drove through Minsk. Since the breakup of the Soviet Union, of which Belarus had been just a tiny part, people had little money. It was difficult to find any food to buy. As Barbara looked out of the window, she could see queues of people standing in front of small kiosks on the edges of the pavement, hoping to purchase whatever supplies the shopkeeper had been able to find. One day it might be bananas or potatoes, another day cigarette lighters or razor blades. Planning a meal was impossible.

They parked outside the children's home and Barbara was struck by how much the outside looked like a concrete warehouse. Her heart was pounding and she didn't know what to expect, but inside the walls were covered with murals of the countryside, the floors were spotlessly clean and the air was filled with a sweet scent. Tamara first explained that Igor was outside with the nurses in the garden, then she and Victor started to negotiate the final details of the plan to bring Igor to Britain for treatment. Next, Tamara and Barbara chatted informally over coffee and Belarussian cakes with the help of a translator.

'We have a big family with lots of grandchildren,' said Barbara. 'I look after other children as well.'

Victor added, 'In some ways it will only be a slight change for Igor, he won't be plucked out of his dormitory and into isolation.'

Tamara was delighted to meet the woman Victor had chosen to give Igor a secure home for the months he would be away and showed her visitors around the children's dormitories. She pointed out Igor's cot just before he loped back into the ward. Dressed in a peaked cap and wearing a big brown woollen coat, he looked like a little sparrow. Igor saw Victor and let out a yelp of delight. He raced over and wrapped his left arm around him. This was the man whom Tamara had said was going to give him an arm and make his dreams of being a fire-fighter come true.

The man had lots of bags with him. Perhaps the arm was hiding inside, holding something in its fingertips. Igor undid the zips and buckles and felt around. 'Where is the arm?' he kept saying in Russian. It was the first time Victor had heard him speak. All Igor could find were cuddly toys, which would be lovely to play with later, but at the moment he had a mission. Then Igor saw a lady who looked a bit like Lilya crouching down next to the man and smiling at him. It was Barbara. Over the lady's shoulder was another, smaller bag . . . the arm must be inside that. Igor ran over and the lady let him open the bag. Anxiously he peered inside, but there was no arm. He spoke to the translator in Russian.

'I need the arm. I'm being told off because I can't wash behind my ears properly, and with two arms I'll be able to put the fire engine on another shelf. Someone keeps taking it down.'

Tamara explained to Victor that Igor thought he was going to get a real arm. Then she looked at Igor and said, 'Victor couldn't bring the arm with him. You can go to England with his friend, Barbara, if you like. She will look after you and then they will make you a special arm.'

Igor desperately wanted to go, but it didn't seem fair. He thought for a moment and said in his loud, commanding voice, 'I've already been away to Germany. Someone else should go.'

Barbara studied this angelic little boy chattering away in a confident, loud, deep voice. He was so bright, it was almost as if he shone. He had lovely curly hair and a mischievous grin on his face. Although his face was that of a six-year-old, he was dressed like a baby in little woollen tights. He looked lost. Barbara just knew he had to come and stay with her; he needed the love of a family. She wanted to do everything she could to help him. Because the arrangement was to last only six months, she decided to tackle any problems as they arose.

Igor was so small, just over sixty centimetres (2 ft) tall, but much less deformed than Barbara had expected. She felt there was something almost neat about his missing limbs. He had been equipped with a functioning body that was just different from everyone else's. From her trip around the children's home, and from a previous visit to Minsk, she knew there were other child victims of Chernobyl who were much worse off. After an hour it was time to leave. It was to be three months before Barbara would see Igor again.

Once he was home, Victor contacted Alan Frame at the *Daily Express*. He wanted to book Igor on to a flight to Britain three days after Christmas. The plan was for the boy to receive three months of physiotherapy at Queen Mary's Hospital in Roehampton to prepare him to receive the new arm. But Victor needed to raise some more money to pay for Igor's living expenses for six months and to put some in reserve for his future. Without funding, Igor might have to return to the children's home, where the threat of being forced to move to a mental institution was still hovering. Charitable donations could allow him to go to school in Minsk, or perhaps pay for a future with a Belarussian family who could adopt him. Victor knew Igor was an extraordinary child who deserved to have hopes for the future like any little boy. He thought another newspaper article specifically aimed at raising money for Igor's rescue might give him that chance.

The second article I wrote was called 'Igor's Fight for a Future'. Published on 11 November 1993, it was illustrated with the proud picture of Igor clutching the fire engine Vic Tucker had given him. It explained Igor's hopes of a new arm to put his fire engine on a higher shelf, and on a more poignant note outlined the future he would inevitably face if the charity couldn't help him. The response to the article was breath-taking. Haslemere post office was jammed with letters arriving at the rate of 300 a day. The postman had to deliver them in giant cloth sacks. In the first week alone, Victor received donations totalling £15,000 for the charity to buy medicines for the other children like Igor in Belarus. His phone rang constantly as he embarked on the mammoth task of replying personally to each letter. Victor then carefully folded each one back into its envelope and filed them away in boxes. He wanted Igor to have a record of all the people who had given him a future.

Some of the letters were typed on company writing paper; others were written in biro on notepaper, or on scrappy pieces of paper torn from exercise books. Many of the letters were very touching.

Our seven-year-old son died a year and a half ago of a rare disease and there is still £500 left in the fund raised by local people. We would like to give the money to your cause for Igor.

Alison Sneath, Dartford, Kent

Jane Warren

Dr Tamara Mourashova holding Nastya, another of the Chernobyl victims. Nastya was born with sealed ears and thumbs which branched into two, each with a perfect nail.

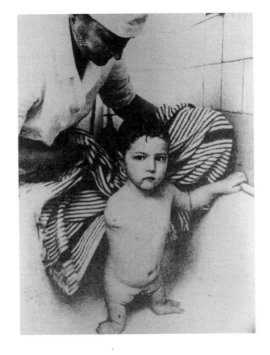

The photograph published in a German Newspaper in 1992, when Igor was four, which inspired Victor Mizzi to find Igor and give him a future.

Igor, aged 6, with his treasured toy fire engine donated by Daily Express *reader, Vic Tucker.*

Igor with Victor on the day after he arrived in England, on January 5, 1994.

Igor surrounded by some of the hundreds of presents and cards from well-wishers which awaited his arrival in Britain.

Rip was the first dog Igor had ever seen. Initially rather nervous, Igor soon came to love this gentle giant.

Larry Ellis

Trying on his bionic arm for the first time, with prosthetist Alan Stephenson.

Barry Gomer

Igor's smiling face shows his excitement at having the arm about which he had dreamed.

Barry Gomer

Here Igor is wearing the first prototype of the boots with 12 cm high cork heels. These were later cut down to 7 cms to enable him to balance more easily.

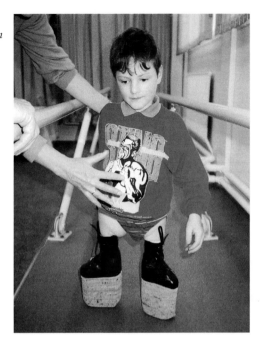

Igor practising to be a fireman on his climbing frame in the Bennett's garden.

Igor met Virginia Bottomley at the local government offices in Godalming in March 1995.

Barry Gomer

The Duchess of York invited Igor, and a group of Belarussian children suffering from cancer, to Princess Eugenie's fifth birthday party in June 1995.

Michael Dunlea

The old woman next to her irradiated house in Bartolomeevka, in the contaminated zone near the Chernobyl reactor, which she refused to leave.

More than 100,000 people have been permanently relocated from their village homes near Chernobyl to soulless high-rise flats in Minsk.

Igor with his "Mummy", Barbara.

I was so moved by Igor's spirit, in spite of all his difficulties, that I felt I must do something to help. Each spring I sow a few seeds such as tomatoes, cucumbers and a few herbs. I always grow more than I need for myself. This year I decided to see if I could sell the leftovers to friends and workmates for a nominal charge. The proceeds from this sale come to £7, for which I have enclosed my cheque. I know it is not a lot, but I am of the opinion that every little helps. I hope you agree.

Mr Wiles, Tunbridge Wells, Kent

I enclose a cheque and hope your appeal will touch many hearts.

John Watson, Bournemouth, Dorset

After reading about Igor I have raised £49.62 from a sponsored swimming event.

Paul Spinks, Frinton-on-Sea, Essex

When you published Igor's photograph a few months ago I cut it out and cried everytime I looked at it.

Mrs Nairn, Bradford, Yorkshire

Some donations were accompanied by kind anonymous jottings and £10 notes. One small scrap of paper simply said in pencil, 'from an 86-year-old age pensioner'. A sheet of cream writing paper bore the words, 'This donation is in memory of my aunt, who died recently and would have wanted to help.' Someone else had written, 'I am on income support and I consider it a privilege to be able to help this beautiful, intelligent little boy in some way.'

Igor had been given a future.

Chapter 6 The Escape

Lilya and Igor spent a happy last afternoon together before he flew to London. They played with his fire engine and walked in the garden of the children's home. Although Lilya had been told Igor would be away for only six months, she knew she wouldn't see him again for a very long time. No one who set eyes on Igor could ever let him go.

Then it was time to say goodbye. Lilya decided not to go to the airport with Tamara, who was flying to England to help Igor settle in. She couldn't trust her emotions. So she picked him up and gave him a good hug. Then she kissed his forehead. He was giggling and smiling, and wanted her to kiss him on the lips. Tears threatened, but she forced them back. Igor mustn't see how sad she was. She must show him only the part of her that was so pleased for him. Igor was excited and anxious in equal measure before he left for England and his sleep was fitful.

He arrived at Heathrow on 4 January 1994. The four-hour flight had alarmed him, especially when Tamara had explained they would be flying over the sea. 'What if the plane falls into the water. I don't have legs to swim,' Igor had said, clutching his seat. But the air stewardesses, with their ritual of serving food from rattling metal trolleys squeezing up and down the aisle, had fascinated him.

Tamara wheeled him into the arrivals hall in an airport wheelchair. Cocooned in a fluffy blue woollen coat, he was dwarfed by the bicycle-size wheels. His eyes were wide with excitement. He'd rarely been in a wheelchair before, so it was quite an adventure. A television crew shone their lights and pointed their big black cameras and fuzzy sound-booms at him. 'Thank you. Thank you,' he said in English, words which Tamara had taught him on the plane. Barbara gave him a hug and Victor popped a red Christmas hat with a white bobble on his head. There was a press conference at the airport, but Igor was more interested in the toy car Victor had given him than in the cameras. As Victor answered questions, Igor investigated. He opened the doors of the vehicle and popped it on the seat of the wheelchair. He opened the bonnet and examined the engine, oblivious to the flashing cameras.

It was nearly midnight when they reached Farncombe, fifty-six kilometres (35 miles) from the airport. Barbara carried Igor upstairs to the first bedroom he had ever known. There was a special surprise waiting for the little boy who was used only to the stark, anonymous surroundings of a hospital ward: his own racing-car bed. Bright green, it even had a handpainted number plate that bore his name. There were also mobiles, a coloured patchwork clown and shelves of cuddly toys. Every time Igor looked at the bed, he could hardly believe what he was seeing. He had found himself in a new and enchanting world where people even *slept* in vehicles.

Barbara showed Tamara to her room and watched as she unpacked Igor's bag. A few pairs of tights, a couple of pairs of pants and some socks. They were his only possessions. He had no other toys or books. The bright red fire engine had been left behind with the other children, because the nurses thought he would be back soon.

The next day Barbara, who was wearing a vivid crimson satin shirt, drove Igor to Victor's house to meet the ITV and SKY television crews. Igor was fascinated by the sixteen-kilometre (10 mile) journey to Haslemere. He'd rarely left the children's home before, so the fields, shops, houses and signposts intrigued him, while the speed of the cars on the A286 was exhilarating. But danger lurked inside Victor's house. A large black wolf sat in the hall. Igor was terrified by the colossal woolly creature, who was bigger than he was. He had never touched a dog before and grabbed hold of Tamara for reassurance. 'This is Rip,' said Victor. 'He is a very gentle dog.' Igor regarded the black furry mountain. Rip regarded him. Then the eight-year-old Labrador/wolfhound ambled over and laid down in front of him. Igor was nervous, but he carefully reached out his hand and touched the dog's soft tummy. The calm giant didn't flinch.

Victor scooped Igor up and sat him on a sofa covered in Christmas packages and the hundreds of letters which had arrived for him. Igor's keen eyes were interested in everything around him: the ringing telephone, the television cameras, the snooker table. He talked rapidly in his strong, confident voice as the cameras filmed him. 'When I grow up I'm going to drive a car and I'm going to drive it so fast that none of your policemen will be able to catch me,' he said earnestly in Russian. He slapped his leg to call Rip over for a biscuit, then he slithered off the sofa and shuttled up and down the room so fast in his excitement that the cameramen had to ask him to slow down so they could film him. He was fascinated by Victor's collection of over 200 ornamental owls arranged on shelves which reached from floor to ceiling. There were wooden ones, fluffy ones, owls with clock-faces that ticked, ceramic ones and stones painted with the wide eyes, pointed ears, sharp beaks and distinctive feathers. Igor turned cartwheels on the cream-coloured carpet, he was so happy.

A few days later it was time to go to Queen Mary's Hospital in Roehampton for the first appointment to see about his bionic arm. All Igor's friends went with him: Victor, Barbara, Tamara and Vic Tucker.

Most boys of six are preoccupied with soccer and video games. They race down the football pitch or coordinate the controls of their hand-held computer games with ease. They take mobility and dexterity for granted. Igor longed to experience such freedom, but he was equally excited at the prospect of being able to wash his own face properly or tie his own shoelaces.

Hugh Steeper Ltd have been Britain's leading artificial limb-makers for seventy-five years. They have supplied prosthetics to thousands of people, including the victims of both world wars, as well as the Falklands and Northern Ireland conflicts. They have thirty branches in the UK and four overseas and are the only upper-limb manufacturers in Britain. Their main unit is a single-storey building at Queen Mary's, where a maze of fitting rooms and offices snakes along a corridor which leads to the workshop. Igor peered into the open doors as Barbara tried to coax him along, but he couldn't believe what he was seeing. In each room were perfect pale-skinned hands, legs, arms and feet. Some of them were resting on desks, others were mounted on the wall or stacked on shelves. It felt like a wonderland of possibilities.

Igor said hello to Bob Taylor, the managing director of Steeper's, who had agreed to treat him for free when he had heard about his plight from Vic Tucker. Then he met the consultant in rehabilitation medicine, Dr Sellaiah Sooriakumaram, who picked him up and gently popped him down on a paper-covered bed topped with a blue towel. 'Let's have a look at you, shall we, young man,' he said, beaming. Igor knew that Dr Soori, as he preferred to call himself, and his colleagues were the men he had dreamed about, the men in the white coats who would be able to give him a perfect right hand to match his left.

Igor was wearing a T-shirt with a picture of a grinning frog on it. He looked tiny and vulnerable against the backdrop of such a clinical setting. Dr Soori took hold of his strong left arm and Igor sat patiently while he flexed it and experimented with other parts of his body. Then the doctor gently laid Igor down, took his socks off and examined his feet. Igor was ticklish and he giggled. A lot of discussions were taking place about how best to help him, but even though he couldn't understand a word, he was perfectly behaved. He knew it was the only way to be if he wanted to get his new arm. Everyone was very impressed with his spirited good humour. Dr Soori discovered that even though Igor was nearly seven, he was the height of an average two-year old, seventy-six centimetres (2ft 6″) while most children his age were between 105 and 120 centimetres tall (3ft 5″ and 3ft 11″).

Tamara had told Igor that his new arm would be covered with lifelike plastic skin, which to Igor sounded as if he was going to get a real limb. The doctor explained to Victor that in fact the bionic arm would have to be a fairly basic design, but Igor didn't understand anything these adults were saying as they discussed his future. He started dreaming again about all the things he would be able to do with two arms.

'Our experience with children who have complex under-developed limbs is that they do best initially if their new arm is mechanically simple,' said the doctor.

Igor draws himself with two arms and two legs

Igor was already dreaming of being able to scale Barbara's climbing frame to reach the top without help. Then his imagination took him up among the highest branches of an oak tree near Barbara's house. Finally he saw himself perched at the dizzy top of a fireman's ladder, seizing a helpless child with his powerful arms and carrying her back down through the smoke to safety.

'If they are provided with too many functions to control, the arm becomes too complicated to operate,' finished Dr Soori.

But Igor's mind was elsewhere.

Then Dr Soori showed Igor the type of arm that Steeper's would build him. Igor's eyebrows knotted and his smile seemed to fade. He pulled Tamara's sleeve and whispered in her ear. 'He thought he was going to get a real arm . . . like his other one,' she said.

But Igor soon cheered up. He seized it and shook hands with it. And he was quick to point out that what he was being shown was a left arm – and he already had one of those. He put his hand inside the closed bionic fingers, then he examined them minutely from every angle. He tried to put the arm on, but it was much too large and didn't fit his shoulder, so instead he worked the buttons which were positioned near the shoulder. They opened and closed the fingers of the 'Scamp' hand, which Steeper's have been responsible for developing. Igor smiled with excitement and put his ear next to the servo motors to hear them humming as the fingers moved.

Igor was then X-rayed. Afterwards, Dr Soori had good news. 'Igor can definitely make good use of a bionic arm. And we think we might be able to do something for his legs.'

Igor could propel himself forward by rocking from one foot to the other and pushing himself along with his arm. It was a surprisingly efficient way of getting around and he could build up considerable speed. The action looked effortless as he gambolled away, his little legs revolving like cartoon helicopter blades, a huge smile on his face. But from a medical point of view, Igor's unusual legs were the biggest problem. The doctors at Steeper's had seen legs like Igor's before, in the 1960s and 1970s, when they had treated Thalidomide children. (Thalidomide was a drug taken by pregnant women which had devastating side-effects. Their babies were sometimes born with malformed flipper feet like Igor's and missing limbs.)

Steeper's decided on a simple approach to begin with. They planned to design a pair of special platform boots which would increase Igor's height by thirteen centimetres (5 inches) as well as distributing the load more evenly on his foot. He was walking on the back of his heels, rather than transferring the load across his feet, which could lead to ulcerations. But the specialist faced a dilemma. Igor was very mobile, so he didn't want the shoes to hinder his ability. At the same time, Dr Soori thought that Igor would benefit from being a few centimetres taller. The crucial question was how high the platform soles could be without being more of a hindrance than a help. When the specialists had seen how Igor coped with the proposed shoes, and after he had grown a little more, they would have a clearer idea about more advanced options for the future.

Then Dr Soori pressed Victor to apply for Igor to stay in Britain longer. 'The boots will take longer than six months to design. We are so impressed with him that we want to help him. Is it possible to extend his visa indefinitely?' It was just as Igor's nurse Lilya had predicted. Victor said he would talk to the Home Office and see what could be done. More appointments were booked before Igor was driven home, waving at the magical men in their white coats.

After only a week in Britain, Igor was adapting well to life outside the hospital ward in Minsk. He was fascinated by shopping at Sainsbury's in Godalming and insisted on loading the trolley with kiwi fruit and melons. Mealtimes were a constant surprise. Food was an overwhelming fascination, which pleased Barbara, as she was keen to feed Igor up. She knew he was in urgent need of nourishing, vitamin-rich meals. When

Barbara opened the fridge, Igor was amazed at the amount of fresh milk sitting inside glass bottles. In the children's home, milk had always been a great luxury, like eggs and butter, which we all take for granted.

In Minsk, Igor had hardly ever seen fresh fruit and vegetables, so he would stare at the fruit bowl on Barbara's kitchen table, mesmerized by the different shapes and colours. The children's home had been able to supply only apples, and just once a month if he was lucky. Soon Barbara discovered that Igor particularly liked grapes. When she gave him a bunch, his face would light up; she said it felt like giving him the world. Igor's mind was filling up with new flavours, textures and smells at the same speed as his tummy was filling up with new foods. For his first Sunday lunch, Barbara served roast chicken with roast potatoes and all the trimmings. Igor was hypnotized by the sight of a plate with so much food on it. He kept offering his plate round. 'In the dormitory everything is shared,' Tamara explained.

Barbara would give Igor the same food as the rest of the family, but he wouldn't automatically pick up a knife or fork, as he was so used to eating with a spoon. For the first few weeks, he would hesitate before deciding what to try. Breakfast was the hardest meal of the day. Igor had never seen ready-sliced bread, yoghurts or cereals, and he wasn't particularly keen on the crunching sensation of Cornflakes or Rice Crispies. Each morning Barbara would pour him a little bowlful from a different packet as a test, making a mental note of the ones he seemed to like. His favourite foods, beside fruit, were fish and pork sausages.

In every other way Tamara was looking after Igor and Barbara kept a low profile. This seemed the best approach to help him adjust to all the new sensations of Western society. Igor wasn't used to sleeping in a room by himself, so Barbara moved Tamara's bed into Igor's cheerful room, next to his racing-car bed. Every night, Igor asked Tamara to kiss him goodnight and to bless him. Igor would then say, 'God bless me in my sleep.' Gradually Tamara began to prepare Igor for her departure. She told him she would be leaving, but he would be well looked after by these kind people. Igor felt very secure in Barbara's home and he knew Victor loved him. He was the man who had been able to make his dreams come true. He felt full of hope about the new limbs he had been promised.

Igor's comment to the television cameras when he first arrived in Britain, about wanting to drive a fast car, had been translated into English when the news bulletin was broadcast and had inspired viewers' generosity. Within a week he had received several remote-control cars and he quickly learned to operate the joystick efficiently with his one hand. He would then spend hours thoroughly absorbed with a car that didn't need pushing along the floor. Among the letters he received was one from two sisters aged seven and nine. They wrote: 'We have saved our sweets' money. Please use this for Igor and children like him.' Sixty pence in coins was jingling about at the bottom of the envelope.

A week later, Igor made his second trip to Queen Mary's Hospital in Roehampton. Alan Stephenson was the prosthetist orthotist who would design the bionic arm. Igor liked him immediately. He was a tall man with a permanently smiling face and floppy hair. He had to take a plaster-cast impression of Igor's shoulder, so the boy took off his T-shirt and Alan wrapped his little body in green paper to stop him getting soaked. Igor had to concentrate. He needed to keep still, but the drips of water were chilly. He knew that after the plaster-cast fitting, he must be patient and wait for the arm to be made. First, Alan would have to design the platform boots in order to determine the length of the new arm, so he measured his feet as well. Alan was delighted with Igor's interest in the different processes.

Tamara had planned to stay four to six weeks in Britain. But one morning, nearly three weeks after she had arrived with

Igor, there was a phone call from the children's home in Minsk. An urgent funding meeting had been called by the local government and she had to go back to argue her case for a bigger budget. Within forty-eight hours she was gone, but before she left she gave full authority for Igor's welfare to Victor, on behalf of Belarus. In a document signed by the Belarus consul in London, she gave him complete authority to oversee Igor's medical treatment and look after his interests in Britain.

It was only after Tamara had left that Barbara bathed Igor for the first time. Until then she had never seen him naked. He was initially shy about his body, because he'd been kept in tights for the first six years of his life. Barbara reassured him, carefully bathed him and hid the tights away. She dressed him in underpants, trousers and socks. It was an important moment. Igor was still like an overgrown baby in so many ways. The next few months would see him develop into a boy. Barbara wanted to give him the opportunity to become independent and develop his already vibrant personality.

Barbara always made sure that Igor was dressed before the other children she looked after arrived each morning and she never undressed him until they had gone. She wanted them to see Igor, not his deformities. Igor loved the company of the other children. He was swept up by their responsive chatter, joined in from the first day and asked what all the toys were called. Kirsty made a particular impression. Like the nurse's daughter at the children's home in Minsk, she had friendly eyes and fair hair. She would let him brush it and curl it on his fingers, and he found this comforting and familiar.

Barbara thought that Igor might be unsettled without Tamara, but he didn't appear to pine for her after she left, or indeed for Lilya. He was safe, warm and well fed. Most importantly, he had a racing-car bed and a fleet of electric cars to control. The thought of the tin cot in the dormitory was no match for all that. Although he sometimes missed the old familiar faces, he tried to ignore the sad feeling he had early in the mornings. He knew what he had to go back to and it didn't compare. In his own mind, he believed that damping down and ignoring the past would give him the best possible chance of remaining in this new, exciting present. He worried that if he seemed to pine for his former life, someone might feel a temptation to return him to it. Soon he had managed to almost completely switch off thoughts of the children's home. His early life in the institution had created a strong sense of survival. If his attitude seemed a little cold, it was hardly surprising given what he had been through.

Back at Queen Mary's for the third visit, Alan explained to Igor that he planned to give him an arm made of lightweight plastic. It would enable him to hold his cutlery and toys. Alan knew Igor would find life much easier if he could grasp things. It would allow him to keep a firm grip while his strong left hand moved them around. Igor would be able to seize a tube of toothpaste in his bionic arm and gently unscrew the cap using his own fingers. He would be able to clutch a felt-tip pen in his new hand and pull off the lid with his natural hand. As the years went by, Igor's bionic arm would have to be updated to keep pace with his growth.

But Alan faced a considerable challenge if he were to give Igor the arm he craved. Artificial-limb technology is a complex enough procedure, but the potential problems and difficulties in design multiply as more and more of the arm needs to be replaced. Igor needed not just a hand but a wrist and an elbow too. Alan explained that the arm would be fitted with an electronic hand to allow the fingers to gently open and close. 'You will have to learn to move your shoulder just the right amount, and in the correct direction, to make the fingers obey your instructions.'

Igor couldn't wait. He was brimming with excitement.

Chapter 7 The Arm

A special bond between the abandoned child and his foster mother had begun to develop. Barbara understood only a few words of Russian and had no time to learn. She needed Igor to learn English, so she treated him as if he didn't talk at all. They began to communicate by sign language and drawing pictures. If they were going for a walk, she would walk her fingers along the table-top during breakfast. If she was driving him somewhere, she would say '*machina*', which means 'car' in Russian. To prepare him for where they were going, she would do a drawing. If it was a trip to the beach, fifty kilometres (30 miles) away on the south coast, her drawing would show the sea with a sailing boat bobbing about on crested waves. From her sketches, Igor would know which clothes to wear. If it was a visit to the park, she would sketch trees, a duck and a pond. Igor particularly enjoyed the ducks. He loved to watch them swimming freely on the pond. He hadn't known birds could be tame, having only ever seen a rather depressed parrot in a cage.

Barbara took Igor everywhere with her, chattering away to him constantly so he could familiarize himself with the sound of the English language. She was amazed at how quickly he started picking up words and how much of her conversation he seemed able to understand. She taught him to count, using her fingers to reach up to ten. But Igor joked he could count only to five, because he had only one hand. As Igor was only 'borrowed', Barbara didn't have a natural mother's anxiety and treated him just like a normal boy. Even going out in public was a treat. Because of all the publicity about his arrival in Farncombe, Barbara found that rather than staring at him, people were coming up and saying, 'Hello, Igor.' No one treated him as an oddity or asked who he was. Instead, he swiftly became a local celebrity.

In the post office Barbara would lift him up to stand on the counter and tell him how many stamps to ask for. He would mimic her sounds in his gruff Soviet/Surrey accent and smile at the lady behind the glass barrier. He would help Barbara to stick the stamps on envelopes and she would carry him so he could post them in the pillar box. He didn't feel phased by any of these new experiences, just fascinated.

Barbara had begun to realize what a truly remarkable little boy he was. She would watch him charging around her house like a little monkey, using his arm for balance. He was so active and independent that at times she found herself forgetting his disability. She certainly had to do nothing more for him than for any other seven-year-old. Although his eyes were permanently out on stalks, nothing phased Igor. He certainly didn't consider letting his disabilities stop him doing anything he wanted. Barbara also loved his innocence; he was so rewarding. She gave him a bright red balloon on a string one day and he gazed at it for ages in wonderment – he'd never seen such a thing before. She adored the way he poured enjoyment into everything.

After only a month in Britain, Igor was already speaking whole sentences in English. He was fascinated by every step towards an arm. During the next of his weekly visits to Queen Mary's, Alan placed a plastic cap made from the plaster-cast impression on Igor's shoulder. 'That's a pretty good fit,' he said proudly and marked the cap with a chalk line where it would have to be cut.

By now a television crew was filming Igor's quest for his new bionic arm. Victor Mizzi had always felt there was a story to be told about the courage of Igor. Through an acquaintance, he was introduced to the production company Zenith North, which was very keen to make a documentary about Igor's early life and rescue to the West. They started filming scenes at Barbara's home, in the park and at the hospital.

Two months after Igor arrived in Britain, Victor had good news. The Home Office had granted an extension on Igor's visa. He could stay in England until 25 February 1996 – another two years! It was now critical for Victor's legal relationship with Igor to be properly defined. When Tamara left no-one in Britain had legal responsibility for Igor's welfare. So Victor had to apply to the High Court in London to make him a Ward of Court. This meant the court would take responsibility for Igor's welfare.

When Igor first arrived, Barbara started compiling his life-story book. This was a scrapbook she began for each child she fostered, designed to give some continuity to their life. Igor's contained newspaper articles about the Chernobyl disaster and his discovery by Victor Mizzi, stuck alongside some of his first drawings. But as the bond between Igor and Barbara developed, her commitment to the book waned. Deep down, she had begun to hope that he would never leave.

Barbara told Igor that soon he would have a birthday. He didn't seem to know what this entailed, so she spent an hour explaining that when he went to bed he would be six, but when he woke up he would be seven. She also told him that he would have a birthday party on the great day itself. The children Barbara cared for brought brightly coloured presents, including a fireman's bucket and yet another fire engine. Igor's eyes were as wide as saucers. There were plates of crisps and sandwiches, but Igor was bewitched by the cake with seven burning candles which Barbara placed in front of him. He blew as hard as he could as the other children clapped and laughed. They played games and danced around with balloons, but at the end of the party, as the children were leaving, he started handing his presents back. Barbara explained they were his to keep and he proudly carried them to his bedroom as if they were diamonds.

At the end of March Igor went to Queen Mary's again, this

time to be laced into his new elevated orthopaedic boots. They looked like way-out platform shoes from the 1960s. They were made of shiny black leather, with a thick wedge of a heel made of cork and a rubber sole. Although they were light, they did look rather dramatic, but they were just a prototype. Alan Stephenson lifted Igor up and gently put him down next to a walking *barre* – two adjustable low poles at Igor's shoulder height which stretched the length of the consulting room. Igor felt his tiny legs buckling beneath him and he adjusted his weight so he could stand upright. He made a tentative step, holding on to the *barre*, but felt he was tipping backwards. He leaned further forward and slowly hobbled along, grasping the *barre* for support. After a number of tense trips back and forth, he dared to take his hand off the *barre* and made several quick steps by himself. Everyone watching gasped as he took another, and another, as if he had just taken the first steps on the moon. Barbara crouched down and held out her arms at the end of the *barre*. Igor teetered for the final few steps and melted into a grateful hug in her arms. She was bursting with pride and admiration.

Barbara was a little alarmed by the boots, because for the first time Igor looked as if he was disabled. She was worried people might now pity him. But Igor was grateful for the extra height; he was tall enough to see inside the kitchen drawer and out of the windows. 'I like being bigger,' he announced one day. After a few weeks of wearing them all day long, he had mastered his balance and could walk without a wobble, although he was unable to move as fast as before. He learned to kick a football with the flat side of the boot, and once kicked so hard that the ball flew into the air and smashed a window in Roy's garden shed. Igor was open-mouthed at the sound of breaking glass, but was secretly rather elated at his ability to create such drama with his solid new boots.

He liked to wash them, inside and out, and lovingly buff them up to a shine worthy of a chief fireman; within a few weeks, he had used up three tins of shoe polish. The boots also allowed him to ride his sturdy push-car. If he sat on the yellow plastic seat without the boots his feet were off the ground, but the boots were like giant paddles which grazed the pavement. Igor could confidently propel himself along, lifting them off the ground like wings as he coasted down inclines on the pavement outside Barbara's house. He felt powerful and fearless. He would swing his legs off the push-car and stride around, but within a few weeks the boots began to feel tight. Igor was frustrated when he looked at his left foot. The larger of his two toes was growing disproportionately fast compared to the other one. It was like a long finger which protruded meaninglessly and barred effortless movement. 'Cut it off, cut it off. Have you got big scissors?' he asked Barbara. Wisely, she hid all the scissors in the house in case Igor's frustration and his reputation for getting his own way combined, with bloodthirsty results.

Igor had settled into British life remarkably well, but there were still occasional signs of his early life in an institution. Barbara was often aware of his tidiness, which could border on the fanatical. One day she hurriedly stuffed some of his underwear into his drawer and the next time she looked, it had all been neatly folded into piles and smoothed flat. Barbara also noticed that if she put one of Igor's toys back in a different place, he would move it to exactly the position it had been in before. Pens, pencils, elastic bands and envelopes were going missing. She knew Igor had them, but when she questioned him he responded with a mischievous grin before scampering off. She understood that because he had never owned anything, he thought he had to hide things to prevent them being taken away.

Igor relished the opportunities and excitement offered by his new life. But right from the beginning he was frightened of being returned to his dormitory in the children's home. He decided there was only one way he could stop this happening.

He would refuse to speak Russian. He wouldn't talk to the parties of Belarussian children who visited Victor or Barbara for a month's holiday under the Chernobyl Children Life Line scheme. The adults accompanying the groups made great efforts to talk to him, but Igor remained silent and sullen. The language reminded him of an earlier existence he preferred to forget.

Barbara was aware of the allure of the new distractions in his life, but she was also conscious that continuity was important. Once his English began to develop sufficiently well, she would ask him about the nurses and the other children, but Igor was reluctant to talk. He had told Barbara very little of his life in Minsk. Sometimes the groups of children flying to Britain brought little parcels for him from Lilya, containing chocolates and story books. Igor couldn't help but tell Barbara about his Lilya and her cuddles and the way she softly sang to him at night. 'Lilya is my granny,' he explained. 'She has grey hair and soft skin.' Lilya wanted Igor to write to her. But he felt torn between his love for her and his fear that writing would somehow spoil everything and mean he'd have to go back. So Barbara wrote instead. Airports also presented a problem. Igor wanted to believe his foster mother wouldn't send him back, but how could he be certain? He was fearful of going to Heathrow airport to meet visiting children. Sometimes he would just march sulkily upstairs, take off his clothes and get into bed when Barbara announced they were going to the airport. But gradually, she was able to build up his confidence. Then in April, Barbara and Roy began talking about their annual two-week holiday to Spain. Igor was invited, but he felt hesitant. Barbara had told him he would have to travel on an aeroplane, but this symbolized only one thing to him – the flight from uncomfortable memories. Eventually, though, he put his trust in Barbara and clambered up the steps of the plane by himself for the two-week holiday by the sea, whispering 'Spain' under his breath.

In July, Igor's bionic right arm was ready for the final fitting. Its length had been calculated so that it would be suitable for wear both with and without the boots. With the boots it would be long enough to reach out and touch the ground, without them it wouldn't scrape the pavement. Alan slid the arm on to Igor's shoulder. There were straps which tucked around his other shoulder to make the arm secure and Velcro buckles to fasten it tight. The arm was heavy – it weighed 1.35 kilos (3 lbs) – but Igor was determined to master the intricate movements which Alan showed him. Moving his shoulder blade would exert a pull on a cable and this would make the fingers of the electronic hand close tightly. Relaxing his shoulder would make the fingers open. He was told that eventually the intricate movements would become second nature.

Igor played a game with his new arm. He slid his own fingers into the open palm of the plastic hand and made the fingers shut, quickly pulling his own hand away before his fingers were trapped. Then he positioned his new hand over a sheet of paper, carefully closed the fingers and picked it up. He hopped up on his black boots, walked to the other end of the room, sat down and slid a pen between the new fingers. Holding it tight, he pulled off its lid with his natural hand. Then he tried to write, but his new hand was at the wrong angle. To rotate its position, Igor had to grasp the new wrist and twist it around. He was then able to make his first ever tentative marks on paper with his right hand. Next Igor switched the pen to his natural hand and effortlessly sketched two pictures of himself. One showed him on the way to hospital with only one arm, the other showed him with two arms.

Igor's new elbow wasn't electronically controlled. If he wanted it to bend, he had to move the lower arm to any position he chose. Pressing a button would fix it there. If Igor found it easy to cope with the new arm, the team promised they would be able to provide additional functions for him. If he wanted an electronically powered wrist or elbow, they

Igor going to hospital with one arm, and going home with two

would be able to add one. But the technology would be expensive: such an arm would cost over £4,000. After two hours' experimentation, Igor had a request. 'Can I take it home?' he asked. 'I want to cut my sausages.'

Before he let Igor leave with the new arm, Alan Stephenson turned his attention to the swiftly growing toe. He decided this was the perfect excuse to refine the shoes. Thirteen-centimetre (5 inch) platforms were too high and Igor was finding stability difficult to achieve. He liked the height, but it was to be surrendered to attain better balance. Alan decided to cut the height of the heels by five centimetres. The lower heels would allow Igor to move faster. Igor matter-of-factly asked them to get out their scissors and cut off the offending digit.

Three months after Igor's arrival in Britain, Barbara and Victor began to think about his schooling. Igor had had some English lessons from a home tutor supplied by the local education authority and was able to hold proper conversations and to enjoy *Peter Pan*, his favourite story, which Barbara would read to him over and over at night. But she knew that if Igor was to stay in Britain, the authorities would expect him to be in full-time education. Teaching him at home wasn't an option because Barbara had no training. Only a school could do the job properly. Barbara and Victor considered the possibilities for a while, but when it was clear that Igor was going to stay in Britain beyond the six-month limit of his first visa, his education became a priority.

Igor was seven years old but had never spent a single day at school. Not only that, but he had no idea what school was like – or even what it meant. He had been raised in a ward where every daily activity, apart from walking in the garden with Lilya, had taken place in the same confined space. Although he was used to having a daily routine broken into organized chunks for eating, sleeping, dancing and playing, he had never had to move more than a few metres to do all these things. The other children who shared this rota of activities with him had been virtually silent, so Igor had never heard the noisy excitement of a classroom or playground. His only conversations had been with Tamara, Lilya and the other nurses when they had the time. Structured schooling was vital. Precious time in Igor's development was still ticking past.

Thirteen kilometres from Farncombe was the small village of Badshot Lea. On the crossroads in the centre of the village was Badshot Lea County Infant School, where 110 children, aged from four to seven, were divided into four classes in a pretty Victorian brick building. Although it was a mainstream school, it had a special needs unit attached for physically handicapped children. Fifteen or twenty of the pupils at Badshot Lea had problems such as communication difficulties, visual impairment or cerebral palsy, an illness which makes it difficult to coordinate speech, arms and legs properly. These special children had some lessons with everyone else, but when they needed a little extra help they went into the unit for individual tuition.

Although Barbara knew it could work well, she was initially hesitant. She wasn't certain that Igor should be segregated and made to feel different. She wanted him to have the opportunity to be as ordinary as possible, because she recognized his intelligence. One day he had followed Roy outside and watched, absorbed, as he replaced the brake pads on the front left wheel of his car. As Roy began on the right-hand wheel, Igor, who had never seen tools before, handed him each one as he needed it. Gradually, Barbara realized that the presence of the special needs unit meant that other children in the school would be accustomed to seeing physical handicaps. So she changed her mind. If Igor attended this school, it seemed unlikely that he would be stared at or picked on, and if things did get too much for him, there was always the reassuring sanctuary of the special needs unit to retreat to.

During the summer of 1994, while Igor's future was being planned, Victor Mizzi drove to the school and took an assembly. The children sat cross-legged in their uniform of red sweatshirts and grey skirts and shorts. They listened goggle-eyed as Victor showed pictures of the youngsters from Igor's children's home, including an enlarged photograph of Igor, the size of a newspaper front page. Victor explained that there had been a terrible accident in the Soviet Union and hundreds of children were living in state orphanages. 'They don't have the things you take for granted,' said Victor. 'You can brush your teeth in the mornings, but they haven't got any toothpaste. Your mummy picks you up if you fall over, but they don't have mummies to cuddle them when they cry.' He also told them that a boy called Igor had recently arrived in Britain to receive a bionic arm. The children asked a lot of questions. One boy wanted to know if the arm would rust if Igor went out in the rain. The children were keen to help, so Victor asked them to collect useful gifts, such as toothpaste and soap, which he would send to the children's home in Minsk. Over the next week, several large cardboard boxes in the school secretary's office filled up with the gifts the youngsters brought in.

Near the end of term the headmistress, Mrs Norman, told the pupils that after the summer holidays they were going to have the little boy from Minsk joining them. She reminded them that Igor had no legs and only one arm. She knew it was important that when Igor first arrived in the playground, the other children didn't stare or flock round him. The children had always been sensitive with pupils who looked slightly different, so she hoped her explanation would do the trick.

Chapter 8 The Teacher

One Monday morning in September 1994 it was time for Igor's first day at school. The television company, Zenith North, had arrived early to film this momentous day in his life, footage that would eventually be broadcast in their documentary. Barbara pulled back the curtains in his bedroom and leaned over Igor, who was pretending to be asleep in his racing-car bed and trying to ignore the cameraman and soundman, who were tiptoeing around in his room with their whirring equipment. Barbara eventually coaxed him out by tickling his tummy. Igor went into the bathroom and pulled his blue plastic step up to the basin, climbed aboard and did his teeth, laughing at the film crew now crammed into the small space by the corner of the bathtub. Igor dressed for school all by himself and Barbara fitted his bionic arm, carefully rolling down the right sleeve of his red school uniform sweatshirt with its white logo. Igor had been practising hard with his bionic arm all summer, but it wasn't quite what he had expected. No one had explained to him how heavy and hard it was going to be. But Alan Stephenson had reassured him that it was only the first prototype and the technology would improve with further refinements.

In the kitchen, with minutes to spare before the taxi arrived to take him to school, Igor asked for a pen and paper. By now he felt oblivious to the film crew; he had more important things to attend to. Barbara had taught him to write his own name and he painstakingly inscribed the four letters on a piece of cardboard. Then he called out, 'Barba, how do you write love?'

'Igor, we haven't got time for all this,' she replied.

He felt crushed and repeated her name. She bustled over and quickly wrote the word in biro. Her eyes, out of necessity, remained half fixed on the clock.

'Barba, how do you write Barba?' he inquired.

'Igor, you're going to be late.' She added her name to the cardboard and shook herself as she suddenly realized what he had asked her to write. Yes, it was a token of security which he wanted to leave at home during his first day at school as a permanent marker of his existence. But he had also dictated an astonishing declaration of love.

Minutes later, sitting in the car with the cameraman and speeding to the school, Barbara asked him, 'What are you going to say when the teacher asks your name?'

'Igor,' he said in his deep voice.

'You have to say, "My name is . . ."' Barbara corrected him.

'My name is Igor,' he boomed, but he was feeling rather nervous when, five minutes later, Barbara led him through the gates of the gabled brick school. In fact, there were hundreds of butterflies flapping madly inside his tummy on top of his breakfast. He clung to Barbara's hand, his heavy plastic arm weighing down his shoulder. All the other children had gone inside. He looked back. The film crew were waving goodbye to him from the gate as they finished filming. Barbara led him in through the double doors, along the corridors and into a bright room with a vast sand tray and lots of pictures on the walls. This looked like an exciting place to be. As he said goodbye to Barbara, most of the butterflies had magically fluttered away. Soon he was absorbed in making sandcastles.

The teachers had decided that Igor should go into the reception class with the four- and five-year-olds. Certainly, they were a similar height to their new classmate and, like them, Igor had arrived without basic number or letter skills. The aim was to teach him the vital nuts and bolts of spelling, counting and writing. They also thought that a less formal classroom, with play equipment, sand and water, would be a gentler

79

introduction to school, rather than joining children of his age who already confidently knew the ropes.

Igor had enough rudimentary English to make his needs clear and to understand his teacher, Mrs Newport, and her simple instructions. Within a few days he was feeling tremendously confident as the taxi pulled up outside number 27. He would rush out with his school rucksack, yelling, 'Bye, Barba,' over his shoulder as he disappeared up the short drive for more drawing, playing and learning. There was so much to do compared with the orphanage in Minsk, where every day had seemed the same. It was a wonderful experience, getting away and playing with other children. He wanted to join in and try anything. But sometimes he missed Lilya.

For the first few days the children did stare at Igor. They had never seen a child with legs like his. Some of them thought they should offer to carry his bags, but Igor didn't like them crowding around, looking at him. He wanted to play football or chase with the boys. So he did. Gradually the novelty factor wore off, just as the headmistress had predicted.

There was a discreetly enforced rule that boys and girls were discouraged from taking their toys to school, but Igor loved bringing things in to show the other children. Usually he would bring in one of his growing collection of small model cars and fire engines. He delighted in explaining all the details with a smiling, happy confidence. He would patiently show his classmates the miniature steering wheels which made the tyres change direction, and with deft fingers he would gently open the intricately detailed doors and bonnets which opened on tiny hinges. When Mrs Newport saw Igor was chattering away in English about his fleet of shiny vehicles, she decided to encourage his enthusiasm and turned a blind eye to this bending of the rules. He had found his own natural way to learn the English language comfortably and confidently.

Igor had speech therapy lessons once a week to develop his vocabulary, but the best way for children to learn a new language is to be immersed in an environment in which they are constantly bombarded with the unfamiliar sounds and soon they begin to become familiar. Igor was particularly adept at picking up English. In class his teachers made an effort to make the lessons as visual as possible so he would understand what they were talking about. They would also give him a few minutes of extra supervision while everyone was settling down to a piece of work, to ensure he knew what to do. After these straightforward approaches, Igor was conversing easily within a few months.

He was also getting the hang of the school week. One Monday morning he said to Barbara, 'Today's Monday so I've got five days at school. But at the end of today, I'll only have four.' He had also learned to dislike school lunches.

Near the beginning of term, the reception-class children were asked to draw or paint a picture of themselves. Many children faced with this task draw themselves as they would like to be, but Igor sat down with a box of crayons and drew a wonderful picture of his big smiling happy face. He then added all the realistic details about himself: he drew only one arm and no legs. His teacher was delighted, for here was a physically handicapped child who had totally accepted who he was. He was completely at one with himself and the sketch radiated this happiness. In the nine months Igor spent at Badshot Lea, he never once complained about his missing limbs.

He loved to provoke a response in other people, perhaps as an antidote to the time spent in Minsk with children who were unable to interact with his games. He would wave and shout 'hello' to Mrs Newport, and adored being admired for his physical agility. But his natural exuberance soon began to distract the younger children in the reception class. At only four and five, they quickly became overwhelmed by the natural clown three years older who was always performing in their midst. The teachers decided it was time Igor was put among children of his own age. They felt confident that he now had the skills to cope, so after autumn half-term Igor moved into Mrs Reid's class of seven-year-olds.

Mrs Reid had first seen Igor when he visited the school at the end of the summer term and had been struck by his smiling face and exuberant manner. She was on playground duty when he had executed his remarkable set of one-armed cartwheels across the tarmac on his first day. A well-built woman with short fair hair and blue eyes, she wore sparkling dangly earrings and colourful skirts. She and Igor admired each other immediately. He liked her cheerfulness and patience. She was captivated by the way he managed so well despite his physical limitations. He seemed able to adapt his little body to any task in an utterly unselfconscious manner and refused to say, 'I can't.'

Even though he had jumped two classes, Igor continued to have his academic work supervised by the special needs coordinator, Miss Falconer. She kept a careful eye on his progress and made sure he was learning things in the right order. He studied art and science with his mainstream class and went to the unit for maths and English, so he was being given all the help he needed.

One day, Mrs Reid decided to set her seven-year-olds their most difficult task so far in a maths lesson. She thought Igor too was ready for the challenge and would welcome the opportunity to try her special project. Mrs Reid had decided to teach her class about tessellations – shapes which could interlink and be repeated over and over again without leaving spaces between them or any overlapping. It was a complex concept to grasp and Mrs Reid had always had varying success with her young pupils. She wondered how Igor would cope with the intricate coordination of paper and scissors. After the explanation, she set Igor and the other children off on their exacting task.

Igor drew the shape he wanted to use. It was an unusual and rather beautiful design and Mrs Reid was surprised by its complexity. She wondered how he would handle cutting it out and linking it together with its repeat. She watched amazed as he slid the paper to the edge of the table, then wedged it under his wrist, picked up the scissors and used his chin to hold the paper still while he cut out the shape over and over again. He built up a little pile of the delicate paper pieces. Mrs Reid cast her eyes around the classroom. Other children with two hands were making a real hash of the project and screwed-up pieces of paper plopped off desks on to the floor. But Igor was thoroughly absorbed. He coloured in each repeat beautifully, then he picked up the glue and began sticking them down next to one another on a clean sheet of paper. He produced a perfect, neat, tessellated pattern with no gaps or wobbly parts. It was the best example the class produced that day.

From then on, Mrs Reid never had to think to herself, 'Now how is Igor going to cope with this?' She knew he would try to tackle anything. He particularly enjoyed physical education lessons. He didn't have to concentrate on an unfamiliar language as he swung from metal rings, hung on to ropes, somersaulted or cartwheeled. He felt agile and confident with his body. Once during a hockey lesson the children were issued with lightweight, full-length hockey sticks. The idea was to move the ball across the playing field, hitting it gently enough to keep it under control. Igor was dwarfed by his hockey stick, but he seized it with his single hand, then sped across the field, the dribbled ball running neatly in front of him, controlled by his delicate nudging on the stick.

Igor had developed a great ease with his imperfect body. When he was changing for PE, he would take off his socks and scamper around in bare feet. Because he was unselfconscious about his unusual feet and the missing toes, the other children hardly gave him a second glance. During movement lessons, when the children danced to music, they were too busy looking at his smiling face to notice his flipper feet and single arm.

The school had a swimming pool for use in the summer, but

every week throughout the year the special needs unit would make a weekly trek by spluttering minibus to the enormous indoor pool at Aldershot. Igor had been nervous of water when he first arrived in Britain, but after his Spanish holiday by the pool, he adored swimming. Although even the children's pool at Aldershot was too deep for him to stand up in without sinking beneath the surface, he refused to be put off. Instead, he would let go of the teacher who had carried him into the shimmering water, launch himself at a float and drift off, cleverly using his feet like fins. Within a few months, he had dispensed with the float and designed his own one-armed splashy front crawl. It was a good thing he always wore goggles and held his breath. He also spent a lot of time propelling his streamlined body along underwater with his muscled arm, exercising his one limb and gazing at the shiny blue tiles. He liked to see everyone's pale legs jumping up and down in slow motion and churning up bubbles. He relished this muffled aquatic environment where he felt weightless and able to glide invisibly past anyone. He was like an otter slicing effortlessly through the funny-tasting chlorinated water. In the changing room one day, as he began undressing, a four-year-old was transfixed by the sight of his missing limbs. 'Where is your arm?' she asked innocently. 'Oh, I knocked it off this morning when I was getting dressed,' said Igor without hesitating.

He was supposed to wear his bionic arm at school, but he struggled with the cumbersome pink plastic. The arm was awkward and heavy. It felt too bulky to keep strapped on to his little shoulder all day long, so he often hid it in his school bag. His teachers encouraged him to learn to use it to eat with a knife and fork, but it was always a battle. The only time Igor looked unhappy at school was when he was trying to cope with balancing a fork in that weighty arm. He was also supposed to wear it during PE lessons to help his balance, but he found it impaired his ability to run, bounce and leap. When the teachers saw he was struggling with it, they relented. They

84

would let him take it off at playtime and Igor, in his crafty manner, would 'forget' to put it back on again afterwards. But he wasn't too worried. A better, lighter arm was being developed for him which would function as a paperweight and hold his exercise books still.

Igor's understanding of English continued to improve, although he found it harder to speak. He loved story-telling time and would sit as still as a heron, concentrating hard on what he was being told without fidgeting. Mrs Reid could tell that Igor really understood the gist of the story because he would eagerly discuss it, and even ask the meanings of unfamiliar words.

He picked up joined-up writing swiftly, helped by a sheet of flat blue plastic lent by the special needs unit. It anchored his paper to the desk and stopped it sliding around. He was also given his own low chair and table in the classroom. It was intended for his safety, but Igor hated being closer to the ground than the other children. He knew he was just as capable of flopping his torso on to an ordinary chair and yanking himself up with his powerful left arm, spinning his little legs up on to the seat. As the year wore on, he would drag a spare full-size chair over to a full-size desk which was at his eye level and sit with the other children. In art classes he would simply stand up on the plastic seat and so would be as tall as the other children who were standing up and daubing paint on to paper.

The children already viewed this new addition to their class as a great asset. Igor was so at ease with his deformities that they related to him as they would to any other child. Igor found making friends effortless because of his confident approach to other people. He was a very sociable child and was swiftly absorbed into groups at school and at home. He also saw no difference between himself and other children and felt no resentment of other children's perfect bodies. Because he behaved like an equal, other children treated him as one. In

Minsk Igor had grown up without the concept of a 'best friend', so his approach was much more straightforward. If someone was fun, Igor would get great enjoyment from them. Neither was he possessive of the children he played with, so he had a wide circle of friends rather than a select few. Barbara noticed that he had a wonderfully trusting attitude towards other people and viewed everyone as his friend, whether they were two or eighty-two. Every week he spoke of different adventures with a mix of new names. His early experiences had given him an immensely independent and self-contained personality. Watching him, Barbara was once again overwhelmed by his apparent lack of emotional problems, despite his unusual start in life.

Igor's greatest love in the world was still fire engines and firemen. He loved to draw and to paint, so his artistic ability was usually poured into intricate pictures of fire-fighting scenes. They were filled with all the colourful details which create a sense of drama: flames leaping into the sky, cascades of water dousing them down and billowing black smoke. Firemen in helmets would climb up the ladders to rescue people trapped on the top floor of houses, or douse the ferocious orange- and red-flecked flames with bright blue water jets. He loved to use a rainbow of different colours. All his art work was nicely presented and neatly done.

One day Igor worked with a partner to make a model tree house to illustrate a story called *A Tree House for Monster*. He relished cutting up and glueing shoe boxes together and designing paper furniture to go inside. He also found sewing surprisingly effortless, despite having only one hand to juggle needle and thread. He was chuffed with the finger-puppet of a mouse he made out of felt. He also contributed towards a class embroidery frieze of the village.

Igor liked working on the school computers and found it very easy to coordinate the different functions on the keyboard in tandem with the mouse. Barbara encouraged his interest, hoping it could lead to a more realistic choice of career in the future.

When it came to stories, Igor was not yet at a stage where he was able to spell and write down a whole sequence of thoughts, so Mrs Reid would ask him to tell her the story behind one of his drawings. Sometimes she asked him to draw a sequence of pictures to tell a story. Of course, there were always police cars, fire engines and houses in flames.

Chapter 9 The Family

As Christmas 1994 approached, Igor had settled very well in year two at school. He was keeping his clowning down to manageable levels and no child had ever dared to tease him. If anyone asked why he didn't have an arm he would simply say, 'I didn't get one.' There were times when he was in trouble for being over-exuberant or disobeying teachers, but no more than any other child. Mrs Reid was delighted with his progress. He was familiar with numbers from one to twenty and was quickly absorbing the vocabulary of mathematical terms; larger, shorter, lighter and so on. Sometimes he needed reassurance after she had set him off on a piece of work. He would stop and quietly bring it to her for her encouragement. Then he would happily return to his desk and continue. By the end of the winter term, he was able to read the early stages of the stage two green books in the Oxford Reading Tree and felt a massive sense of achievement when he read a whole book independently. During music lessons he was in his element. He had a good sense of rhythm and would join in the singing with gusto. He also liked playing accompaniments on the tamborine and triangle.

Igor had spent three months surrounded by normal children from loving homes. It was inevitable that he should begin to crave the intimacy of a family of his own. One day during the Christmas holidays, when the Bennetts' house was filled with brightly coloured tinsel and a statuesque Christmas tree which he and Barbara had festooned with glittering decorations, and Igor was sitting at the kitchen table surrounded by paper and felt-tips, he suddenly announced, 'I've made you a drawing.'

His picture showed a neatly drawn, carefully coloured-in fire engine. Above it, he had written, 'to Mummy and Daddy'. In the children's home Igor had had no concept of families, so this was the first time he had referred to her and Roy in this way. Barbara was amazed. Initially she was surprised he could write the words, but then the inference of what he had written hit her. Igor had become extremely attached to her and Roy. Barbara felt hugely emotional about his expression of affection, but her pleasure was mixed with an equal sense of consternation. She didn't know what the future held for Igor. She was worried by the strength of his attachment to her and Roy. How would the system treat them? Could she allow herself to return his love, secure in the sense that it could be ongoing?

She was aware that it was school that had encouraged him to begin a craving sense of belonging to a family. It had also created a desire in him for information about human relationships. For some time he had wanted to know why some people called Barbara and Roy 'Granny' and 'Grandad'. And when their daughter Debbie was pregnant, he'd ask Barbara hopefully, but without too much conviction, 'Did I go in your tummy?' Barbara had pinched him and said, 'Don't be silly, you've only been in England for a little while.' Igor then persisted on another tack: 'I wasn't born a baby, I was born a boy, ready to come to England.'

More pictures of his 'Mummy' followed, usually with bright green hair, a fashion detail which he quickly discovered was guaranteed to send her swooping on him noisily. When Barbara's grandson Toby was born, Igor's first question was, 'Does he have both arms and legs?' Barbara had recently told Igor in vague terms about his past. 'There was a nasty bang. Your real Mummy lived nearby and a thing called radiation made her ill. That's why you haven't grown properly.' Igor continued to speak only fleetingly of Belarus and in mainly negative terms. Sometimes he would say, 'We have that in Minsk, but not as good.' He was still reluctant to speak

MUM

Russian, but Barbara was aware he needed to be reminded of his culture and was worried that he would forget his native language. Roy had a Russian-speaking friend who came to visit them sometimes, but Igor would stride across the patio-garden, shutting out the horribly familiar words wafting across the paving slabs. 'I'm English, I don't need to speak Russian,' he once spat.

Victor Mizzi realized it would be in Igor's best interests to stay in Britain for a longer period so that he could continue to be helped by Steeper's who had offered to treat him for free. He made an application to the immigration department for another extension to his visa. In March 1995, Igor met his local MP, Virginia Bottomley, then Secretary of State for Health, at the local government offices in Godalming. He embraced her with his strong right arm and she promised to do all she could to help his cause. After this meeting she wrote to Victor:

I would like to say how moved I was to meet Igor last week. The world is full of people who identify problems. Those who decide to take practical steps to improve the circumstances of fellow human beings deserve the highest praise. I would like to send my warmest congratulations to you and all those involved in his care, to whom I hope you will pass on my best wishes: Mr Tucker, Mr Stephenson and, of course, Barbara.

One day Barbara told Igor that soon it would be his eighth birthday. Igor was confused. 'But, Mummy, I've already had a birthday – last year.' Barbara explained that birthdays and birthday parties are actually an annual event. Igor looked glum. When she asked him why, he said he was sad because he wasn't ready to return his toys just yet, so when she told him he could keep them he was delighted. For his birthday treat, Barbara said that he could choose four or five friends to take to Bird World near Aldershot. Igor was very popular and most of his friends were active, tough little boys who loved to kick a football. But among his birthday guests was Sophia, one of the kindest girls in his class. Igor's closest friend was seven-year-old Lee, a quiet, sensitive boy who didn't push himself forward and was always very thoughtful.

Igor went to another, rather special birthday bash in March. The Duchess of York invited him and a group of visiting Belarussian children suffering from cancer to Princess Eugenie's fifth party. It was held at the Royal Berkshire Hotel in Sunninghill, outside Ascot, close to her home on the Wentworth Estate. Large rugs were spread on the bright lawns and Igor sat as guest of honour with Fergie and her daughters, the Princesses Beatrice and Eugenie. They were entranced by the witty little boy as they played with balloons together. There was a massive cake with five candles, a juggler and a clown. When the clown asked for a volunteer for a trick, Igor's arm shot into the air. The Duchess saw her daughters' delight with Igor. From then on, if they complained or were badly behaved, she would remind them about Igor and how he didn't make a fuss, despite his missing limbs.

Victor continued to receive letters and money from people who were reading articles and watching television items about Igor's progress. Victor always replied to each letter, regardless of whether any money was enclosed inside the envelopes. Many letters were from children who found it easy to identify with Igor's lively manner.

On notepaper, with colourful elephants striding across it, a little girl called Charley wrote to Victor in large black hand-writing:

> Dear Mr Mizzi, I have saved up my pocket money and now I have got six pounds. Please could you send the money to the children in Russia. Or buy some medicines and then send it to Russia. Thank you Mr Mizzi. Love from Charley. xxx.

During the holidays, two girls called Katy McEvoy and Emma Perkins held a fete in Katy's garden in Surrey to which Igor was invited. They raised £150 for the charity:

> Dear Mr Mizzi, We had a lovely time yesterday. We were really glad that Igor could come and he had a great time. At the end Igor wanted us to throw wet sponges at him, so we threw gently and he said to throw them harder. But even that wasn't enough for him so he filled a bucket of water and poured it over his head. He also did somersaults and cart-wheels all over the garden. He won on mini golf and made a determined effort on the pinball. We made sure he went home with lots of prizes. We hope that this enclosed cheque

will help to bring over another child from Russia. Yours sincerely Katy and Emma. PS. I might have another fete next year.

Igor joined his foster parents for his second Spanish holiday in May 1995. He practised his swimming strokes under the baking sun and turned a healthy brown. He giggled as he asked the barman for Roy's vodka, but when he returned to school he had an alarming tale to tell his class. With a weighty expression on his face, he recalled how he and the Bennetts had been involved in a dramatic air-sea rescue. They had gone on a boat trip around the bay, but got into difficulties with the heavy sea. A helicopter had picked them up from their sinking dinghy, but as the rescue noose was slipped around Igor's torso it had slipped off because of his single arm and he had nearly plunged into the waves. Igor's teacher, Mrs Reid, anxiously phoned Barbara to see if she was recovering well after her ordeal. Barbara didn't know what she was talking about. The whole story was a product of Igor's fertile imagination – he loved playing practical jokes. When Mrs Reid confronted him, he bellowed with laughter at his power to persuade adults in his new language. She was secretly impressed with his eye for detail.

But Igor was growing reticent about his experiences as a media celebrity. He wanted to be normal like the other children and to blend in as far as possible with them. If someone said, 'I saw you on television,' he would turn his back and walk away. Barbara picked up on this shyness, and stopped showing him the magazine and newspaper articles that were published about him.

Igor's dreams of becoming a fireman remained as powerful as ever. The red toy fire engine that Vic Tucker had given him had been his first real hint of the outside world and its influence continued to hold firm. Barbara encouraged his passion and brought him a yellow plastic fireman's hat. He would scale the climbing frame in the garden, pretending he was at influence continued to hold firm. Barbara encouraged his passion and brought him a yellow plastic fireman's hat. He would scale the climbing frame in the garden, pretending he was at the top of an extending ladder, and the magnificent sound of a real fire engine tearing along the road had him racing to the garden fence. When *Daily Express* photographer Larry Ellis came to take photographs one summer afternoon, he refused to cooperate until we agreed to watch him douse imaginary flames roaring out of his wooden Wendy house in the garden and rescue an imaginary damsel. It didn't matter how many times Barbara gently hinted at the practical problems concerning his chosen career, Igor would not be swayed from his ambition. If she said, 'You've only got one arm,' he would say, 'I'm going to hold the hose.' If she hinted at his little legs, he would simply say, 'I won't drive, I'll be one of the ones in the back.'

One of the most exciting days of Igor's life was when he met the cast of his favourite television series, *London's Burning*, in June 1995. Within minutes of meeting his heroes, he had taken over the London Weekend Television film set. Everyone was moved by his energy and his cheerfulness. Igor had become hooked on the long-running series as soon as he saw it, even before he understood the words. He also took it utterly seriously. When he watched a story that spanned two episodes he said, 'The firemen must be so tired – they've been fighting the fire all week while I've been at school.' One summer afternoon, Victor and Barbara took him to Shropshire for a party with other Chernobyl children. The local fire brigade brought their engine along to show them. It was Igor's third ride in a fire engine; he had already been to the stations in Godalming and Guildford. On each occasion he would sit in the front seat making sound effects and feeling wonderfully proud.

Igor was now the oldest boy at Badshot Lea and at the end of the summer term in July 1995 it was time for him to leave. He had developed an adult-looking face and had a sturdy torso. If he had been blessed with a complete body, the teachers agreed he would have been as tall as the biggest boys at the school. Igor had worked so hard that his year spent in the small village school had really paid off. At the beginning, Barbara had simply hoped that he would enjoy himself and hadn't dared to hope for more than a zero in his National Curriculum Assessment grades. Instead he passed Key Stage One with grade 1 in every subject: reading, writing, spelling, handwriting and maths. This was the same grade as children who had been at the school for three years, not just nine months. Mrs Reid's end of year report glowed with praise:

Igor is a confident, well-adjusted child who enjoys life to the full. He makes friends easily and is friendly with adults and children alike. He is bright, alert and learns quickly. He participates in every area of the curriculum, and has produced some lovely, careful pieces of work. He listens attentively and enjoys offering his own thoughts and ideas. He has persevered with the English language and is able to converse fluently. He loves books and particularly enjoys having stories read to him, and talking about the pictures. Igor is extremely agile in PE and shows no fear or apprehension at all. He compensates for his 'disability' remarkably well and joins in all activities with gusto. Igor has an inquiring mind and has settled into school life exceptionally well. He has done extremely well to achieve Level 1 in maths, reading and writing and I am sure he will continue to make progress when he moves on to the junior school.

Mrs Reid wrote her report with great sadness that she would no longer be able to teach such a bright and inspiring child, whom she had so come to admire.

Igor had found his first bionic arm heavy and somewhat difficult to control, so Steeper's had designed him another one without the electronic hand. It was a cosmetic arm which served two purposes: he could roll down his sleeve over it so he didn't look so disabled and it also made the perfect anchor for all his school work. Resting the arm on the paper, he was able to hold his exercise books perfectly still and draw a straight line. It was a liberation, the ultimate portable paperweight.

In the summer holidays Igor's dream of playing soccer came true when Steeper's presented him with a surprise: his own special pair of custom-built football boots with coloured laces and proper black studs on the soles. He hadn't been able to kick a ball on grass before, because his other shoes didn't grip. Laced into his new boots, he was soon tearing around on the grass outside Queen Mary's Hospital. Igor hoped that he would be able to play real football at his new school. Victor and Barbara were still discussing exactly where his education was to continue.

One day during the holidays, some nine-year-old boys knocked on Barbara's door to ask if Igor could come out to play. She reluctantly told them that he was too small and might get hurt. Twenty minutes later, as she weeded the front garden, she heard cheering and shouting drifting down the road. She put down her secateurs on the grass and stood up, brushing soil off her knees. Igor was perched on a skateboard, whizzing down the centre of the road. The two older boys were running alongside him, ready to catch him if he fell. But he kept his gaze level and his arm outstretched for balance. His little body was flexing like a reed in the wind to help him to steady himself. The skateboard gradually rolled to a halt and Igor jumped off.

During the summer Igor used to visit an adventure playground for special needs children near Guildford. Once he excitedly told Barbara about scrambling up the climbing frame and mentioned his 'friend'. Intrigued, Barbara stayed to watch after she had dropped him off one day. She saw Igor immediately run to the side of a young girl in an electronically powered wheelchair. Igor guided her carefully through the playground, responded by pressing the controls of her wheelchair to pick up speed. Barbara asked a playground worker who the girl was. 'Igor's girlfriend,' was the answer.

In September 1995, Igor started at the William Cobbett County Junior School in Farnham with 400 children aged eight to twelve. He was to be part of the special needs unit there, but would take some lessons with his classmates, just as before. Igor missed his old teacher. After his first day at the new school, he said forlornly to Barbara, 'Why didn't Mrs Reid come with me?'

Igor's new eight-year-old classmates were happy to play football with him. They were tolerant of his needs and indulged him by slipping the ball to him. But Igor wanted more. His ambition was to play with the big boys. One lunchtime, he put his feet into the new bespoke football boots and strode into their playground territory. He nearly collided with one of the twelve-year-olds, who was racing with the ball and didn't see the tiny boy, less than half his height, who was gazing eagerly at the nifty footwork. He just avoided knocking Igor over like a skittle. The big boys booed at Igor and told him to get out of the way. He felt utterly dejected as he shuffled slowly back to the younger boys, cursing his stupid body and missing legs, which made his dreams impossible. Sometimes even playing with friends was a frustration. If he went to give the ball a hard kick, he often fell over when his boots made contact with the ball. Barbara knew it was vital to stand back and let him discover his own limitations, but she didn't always find it easy when he came home miserable.

In October Igor was admitted to a London hospital for exploratory surgery. There was a danger that his little body might harbour a cancerous growth which, although invisible now, might grow into a tumour in the future. It was a nail-biting time. No-one could predict the influence of radiation he had received in the womb, on his body. Victor had contacted Tamara for her permission for the operation to take place, but it was judged to be a great success. The surgeon could find no evidence whatsoever of any potential problems. Barbara, like a good mother, stayed by Igor's side for forty-eight hours before, during and after the operation. Just twenty-four hours after his surgery, he was allowed home. Victor and his wife, Birgitta, came with Valentina, the Belarussian coordinator, to see Igor at home. They expected to find him lying quietly in bed. To their surprise, he was in the sitting room, playing with his toys. As soon as he saw them, he jumped on the sofa and pulled up his jumper to show off the little scar, with no inhibitions at all. For the next two weeks this was normal practice, until Barbara gently persuaded him that he had shown enough people the intimate wound.

In November, Barbara asked Igor if he would like to go back to Minsk for a holiday with her one day. He didn't answer and disappeared up to his room. His fears about being sent back seemed as strong as ever so Barbara felt a short trip in the future to visit Lilya and Tamara would be important for his emotional development. She wanted Igor to get over his anxiety and really learn to trust her. Barbara had grown tremendously attached to Igor and after eighteen months she couldn't visualize life without him. 'He's really my little boy in lots and lots of ways,' she told the documentary film-makers with tears welling up in her eyes. 'Every morning I tell myself, "He's not yours, he's borrowed, you can't love him," but all the logical things go out of the window. There are some children you can just feed and clothe, but not Igor.' She was dazzled by his positive attitude to life, despite his inauspicious beginnings in an institution, and by his self-possessed enthusiasm. It felt as if he had been part of her family for ever. She adored his intense imagination, his impish sense of humour, his eye for detail and his lively confidence. But she had begun to fear that someone might try to take him away from her. So on 9 December 1995, Victor Mizzi approached the High Court in London about this issue. Igor was to reside with

Barbara Bennett for as long as his visa allowed him to remain in Britain. No one could remove him without the approval of the court.

But Victor was still uncertain how long Igor would be allowed to stay in Britain. The months had rolled by and documents about Igor were being tossed between various government departments like a netball. Their old ally, Virginia Bottomley, who had been so moved by Igor when they met, had also been working on his behalf, firing off letters to Home Secretary Michael Howard. But the expiry date on Igor's visa was looming perilously close. Victor spent hours welded to his phone, cajoling and pleading with a variety of civil servants. On 9 February 1996, just over two weeks before his visa expired and Igor's residency visa would have expired, Victor's perseverance paid off. A letter from Virginia Bottomley dropped through the letter-box.

I am pleased to send you a copy of the letter I received this morning from the Home Secretary, the Rt Hon. Michael Howard, QC, MP . . . Igor Pavlovets has been granted leave to remain for a further two years until 25 February 1998. This is good news indeed. Please pass on my best wishes to Igor. Do let us keep in close touch.

Attached was a letter signed by Michael Howard which said, 'At the end of this period Mr Mizzi may reapply on Igor's behalf for further leave to remain when again his application will be given sympathetic consideration.' Victor was overjoyed and felt deeply grateful for British justice and compassion.

Chapter 10 *The Dead Zone*

If Igor were to return to Bragin, the town where he was conceived, he would sense despair. In 1993 I visited his former home in the contaminated area with Victor Mizzi and Chernobyl Children Life Line. The once flourishing rural town lies just twenty-five kilometres (15 miles) north of the barbed wire beginning of the enforced evacuation zone. Many of the houses have been looted and abandoned. The original population of 17,000 has shrivelled to a quarter of that size since people realized that they were living on contaminated land, despite the fact the Soviet government had been feeding them contradictory information after the disaster.

We set off towards the dead zone in a cream-coloured Lada. Purple nylon curtains covered the back window and a small red plastic skeleton dangled ominously from the rear-view mirror. We slipped into the countryside and began charging through huge stands of forests with black hearts looming beneath their heavy canopies. The land felt as flat as the Australian outback. The road, as ramrod straight as a Roman road, stretched long and thin and snake-like into the distance. It tapered away into sand and shrubs at the edges. We negotiated pot-holes the size of bathtubs, but there was no traffic to avoid. As we approached the danger area, people were toiling in the fields, digging and hoeing the deceptively perfect-looking soil, but as we drove on the few scarecrow figures in the fields dwindled. A solitary individual on a bicycle pedalled past, breathing deeply. A horse pulled a cart.

Soon there was silence and calm. We pushed on, deeper into this dead and desolate countryside – these beautiful killing fields. The driver dictated a list of chilling instructions as we approached the dead zone, just thirty-two kilometres (20 miles) from the Chernobyl reactor and our translator interpreted: Do not touch anything. Do not put your hands to your mouth. Do not breathe deeply and, above all, try to stay on the tarmac.

We saw the official checkpoint looming up ahead and tension filled the car. We had no permit to enter the area because it is difficult to get official approval. But as we approached the wooden hut, a bored-looking soldier, waved us through. Teenagers on National Service are often posted to man these bleak outposts. As we accelerated past him, we saw ominous signs stuck to sticks. A bright yellow symbol with three small arrows pointing to its centre carried the words: 'Radiation Danger: It is prohibited to grow and collect agricultural products, to make hay and to raise cattle.' A white sign painted with jagged black letters was staked into the ground next to some trees and read: 'Danger of radiation. Entry and exit prohibited.' The road we were travelling along had been resurfaced in an effort to limit the radiation. For two hours, if you are careful, you are safe.

The land on either side of us is so radioactively hot that when snow falls, it instantly melts on contact with the ground. This is despite temperatures which can reach thirty degrees centigrade below freezing. We had entered hell and yet it was so tranquil that it was difficult to believe the silent menace which has made lethal this once fertile land filled with fields of potatoes and beans. All you can do is look for signs, like the fact that the hay in the fields has not been cut for ten years. It has wilted and now looks like long, untidy hair, laying rotting on the unturned soil. Very soon the feeling of claustrophobia overwhelms you and you begin to panic about what might happen if the car spluttered to a halt. There are pylons but no power, phone lines but no connections; there are no petrol stations, there is no civilization, and all the time your body is clocking up a radiation dose which you cannot control.

The village of Bartolomeevka, 400 kilometres (250 miles) from Minsk, is like a cemetery. It was abandoned in 1989, when the villagers were forced to leave all their irradiated possessions behind. A single narrow road stretches through the centre of this typical abandoned village. Outside one house is a rusting pushchair with a ripped fabric seat. On the overgrown grass in front of another, a hand-turned wooden cot painted bright green, rests at a jaunty angle. Some of the struts are broken and the paint is peeling away. The slatted fences in front of the small hairy gardens have also decayed.

I broke the rules for a moment and picked and poked my way into one of the pretty houses, painted in bright boiled-sweet shades, which were mouldering back into the ground. The front door had rocked off its rusty hinges. The tendrils of botanic invaders had curled and snaked their way in through the broken glass of the hand-carved window-frames. The floorboards had collapsed into the cellars, and floral wallpaper was growing new, unintended mould patterns. In the kitchen there were chipped china cups, bottles and cooking pots standing as they had been left. In the front room lay a pair of small red patent leather shoes, and near the fire grate an unloved dolly with dirty blonde hair and broken legs was reclining in the dust and rat droppings. On the wall above her hung a black-and-white photograph of a little girl with a bow in her hair. The glass was smashed, but the child stared out defiantly through the shards.

As I nipped back on to the tarmac a human creature scuttled from the shadows. The woman, in her sixties, looked like a scarecrow in her tattered brown rags. She told us she hadn't been able to comprehend the idea of leaving the only home she had ever known, so she and her brothers had refused to go and now she was nursing the graves she had dug for them when they had died. She invited us into her disintegrating, irradiated house through a gate in the fence. She had a clay oven where she cooked the turnips and potatoes that she grows. In the corner lurked an emaciated tortoiseshell cat with a backbone like the arch of a coat hanger.

All the while our driver remained alert. The police check car could come at any moment – it makes the rounds of the area and you face arrest if you have entered and stopped without a permit. He glanced at his watch and asked us to run back to the cars. Soon we had left the sombre village, driving on past an abandoned school where all the glass in the windows had been punched to the ground. Ten kilometres further on, two more rag-shrouded elderly people stood in a concrete bus shelter, waiting for a bus which will never arrive. The intense claustrophobia of this area is difficult to convey. It is deathly quiet – no bird sings. The place is both obscenely fascinating and intensely repellent. Just a little while longer, you dare yourself, as you sneak into another house and off the tarmac. One more photograph can't make any difference.

We saw barbed-wire fences, one field away from the road, which signified a dump-site where the land has been excavated and fall-out from the reactor buried in shallow graves. Skeletal cranes stand abandoned and irradiated, rearing their rusty heads into the grey sky.

We drove to within four kilometres (2½ miles) of the border with the Ukraine before turning back and beginning our escape in the softly falling rain. The rain was lucky for us – the area is more dangerous when it is hot and dusty, with a wind which whips contaminated particles into your face. The roads were beginning to convert to greenery, with plants springing up in the cracks. Not everything is dead.

The villagers from pastoral communities like Bartolomeevka have been moved to ugly high-rise blocks in Minsk. Immediately following the disaster, 24,700 people were bussed out after the radioactive dust had fallen on their homes in areas registering fifteen or more curies of radiation per square kilometre. To date more than 100,000 people have been permanently relocated from their homes in areas of ten to fifteen curies. Anyone living in an area with less than ten curies was doomed to stay, despite the health risks.

We visited the micro-districts in Minsk, over 320 kilometres from this contaminated land. They seem to stretch for ever, nine-storey blocks with broken elevators. Outside there is no grass and only a few shops which sell basic food – eggs and bread and pickled onions. Fresh vegetables are unknown. It is difficult for people from the country to adapt to a bland existence on the ninth floor.

Vera Afanasianco is thirty-one. She was one of the last villagers to be resettled with her children, seven-year-old Dimar and ten-year-old Anton. She has few possessions: two chairs, a sofa bed, a cracked vase and an antiquated television with a flickering picture. When her family was relocated from the contaminated area, they were forced to leave everything behind. There are no pictures on the walls and a stale smell fills her two-room flat, which is wall-to-wall linoleum.

'I am terrified my children will develop cancer,' she says, looking dejectedly out across the acres of concrete. 'We had to wait five years in the contaminated area until we reached the top of the housing list. There is not a single day we don't long for our chickens and our home.'

If Igor was at school in Minsk, his education couldn't be more different from the cosy and constructive environment of his school in Surrey. Vera's children, like the other refugees in the drab high-rises, attend schools in the micro-districts. With over 2,000 pupils, these schools are more like education factories. Because of the high demand for lessons and a shortage of money to build new schools, exhausted teachers run two separate school days, with two different sets of pupils. The first lessons start at seven a.m. until two p.m. The second sitting begins at two p.m. and finishes six hours later. Inside School Six, there were vast shadowed corridors down which children zoomed like runaway dodgems. Others lurked outside the front doors, sucking on cigarettes. There was no grass or playing fields beyond the pebble-dash walls, no trees or flowers, just acres of mud and dust. Since 1991 Belarussian school children have been receiving environmental lessons which teach them about radiation. They learn about its characteristics and are taught how to behave safely in contaminated areas.

The deputy headmistress of School Six was surprisingly bubbly and jovial. She was also immensely dedicated. She is paid just £15 a month and out of this the photocopying costs for her pupils have to be drawn. The school has no photocopier of its own and she had just one English language textbook. Because she thinks it vital that her students are given the option of learning English, she has arranged to have some of the larger classrooms converted into several smaller language labs. The wallpaper is badly stuck to the damp walls and peeling at the edges.

But at least this school is not located in a contaminated area. Over 2,000 schools in Belarus are trying to operate in the hot zone. Many of them have no central heating, no running water, no sewage system, no sports hall and no canteen. Many of them, not surprisingly, are desperately short of teachers.

The health impacts of the Chernobyl disaster are difficult to measure, but the government estimates that there are currently over one million children deformed, damaged or diseased as a consequence. Between 1990 and 1994, many types of health disorders among the children of Belarus increased. Recent Unicef figures show that defects of the heart, circulatory and nervous systems have gone up by 43 per cent, disorders of the digestive organs by 28 per cent, disorders of the bone, muscle and connective tissues by 62 per cent, anaemia by 10 per cent and asthma by 48 per cent. Cancer of the thyroid is one of the most serious problems. Between 1966 and 1985 twenty-one children had surgery, but between 1986 and 1994 that figure swelled to 329 operations.

'These figures will continue to climb every year for the next

400 years,' predicts Dr Reiman Ismailzade, who runs a children's cancer hospital near Minsk. 'I am seeing types of cancer that before I only read about in textbooks.' Before the meltdown, his hospital did not even exist, but today medicine is in desperately short supply. 'Resources are so slim here that if we use a needle only a thousand times we consider we are being extravagant,' he says. When Victor Mizzi hands him a suitcase of pain-relieving cancer drugs, the doctor immediately calls his staff. Within ten minutes the first children are being injected with anti-nausea serums.

Igor, despite his physical disability, is one of the lucky children of Chernobyl. He has been given a new life. Most children have no choice but to watch their health deteriorate as they grow older. A 1993 health survey examined 500 Belarussian children and found only one to be completely healthy.

Yet the only official monument in Belarus to the ongoing tragedy is in a park in Minsk. Shaded by trees, three lumps of highly polished stone the size of coffins face the road which scars the park. Every year, on 26 April, the anniversary of the disaster, these jet-black stones are shrouded in carnations and roses. Loudspeakers from a van blare out rousing music and a clutch of people stand with lighted candles. Speeches are made, people cry, the music plays. A few hours later the memorial is once again deserted.

Epilogue: The Future

As this book goes to press, Igor is just two weeks short of his ninth birthday on 29 March 1996. He speaks almost perfect English and is a joy to spend time with. His left arm grows more powerful by the day and he no longer uses it as a third leg. Instead, he delights in arm-wrestling his visitors. Of course, he always wins. Unknown to him, he is bringing attention to the plight of the other children of Chernobyl, left behind on contaminated land, and has become a symbol of their courage.

Barbara's house is filled with Igor's favourite toys. But he still asks after his first red fire engine, which is with the other children at the orphanage in Minsk. Many of his new possessions, like the plastic filling station, are designed for much younger children, but he is unaware of the age difference. He is simply glad that the pretend pumps and dials are at his eye level. Igor is an avid Lego model-builder and the lowest shelf in his bedroom is dedicated to his beautifully crafted Lego scenes of fire stations. He still dreams of being a fireman and his drawings of engines grow ever more precise.

The Carlton documentary about Igor's life, *Igor: Child of Chernobyl*, was shown on Tuesday 6 June 1995. Igor stayed up late to watch the hour-long programme, which dealt honestly with human relationships of a very delicate nature. The only part he didn't enjoy was hearing himself singing an improvised carol on Christmas Day. 'I asked them not to put that bit in,' he told Barbara as he hid under the bedclothes. The next morning he went to school as usual. Barbara's and Victor Mizzi's phones began ringing with offers of help and money.

The duty officer at Carlton also confirmed that rarely had a programme provoked so many phone calls. Haslemere post office was once again swamped by 5,000 letters, all inquiring how they could help the children of Chernobyl shown in the film. The result was 150 tonnes of aid donated by pharmaceutical companies, including Blackmore's, and schools which ran appeals for food and clothes. Viewers also organized fundraising activities nationwide, including sponsored walks, runs and rides, gala concerts, bring-and-buy sales and charity dinners. The documentary has since been shown in many other countries and won eight major television awards. The Embassy of the Republic of Belarus, in London, was among the letter writers. Officials there were deeply grateful for the publicity the film had given to the plight of their people. They wrote, 'One of the main values of the film is that ordinary people have not been indifferent to the grief of our nation.'

Ask Igor if he will return to Minsk and he scratches his wavy brown hair, looks wistful and says, 'Yes, but only for a holiday.' He now feels more secure about airports. Recently he and Barbara drove to Heathrow with Victor, who had forgotten to buckle his seat belt. In the terminal Igor saw two policemen patrolling with guns, so he ran up to them and told them they should arrest Victor. On another visit to the airport he spotted a businessman with a mobile phone and asked if he could use it to call his 'Daddy'. The man couldn't resist the tiny boy at his feet. Igor knew exactly which buttons to press and chatted to Roy for several minutes.

Typical of how he wins over strangers was when he met a fifty-year-old bachelor who almost prides himself on his lack of rapport with or interest in children. Half an hour after their meeting, the pair were engaged in a full-scale battle in Victor's garden. The adult, who is nearly two metres tall (6ft 4ins), lay prostrate on the garden path, peppering the tiny boy with imaginary sub-machine-gun fire, while Igor crept up on him with Action Man and a large stick. Gales of childish laughter filtered into the house for the next hour. The man was amazed by the boy's agility; Igor reminded him of a baby seal scampering across rocks. The man, whom Igor swiftly named 'that big giant', felt this bright little boy had shown him what fun children could be.

At the moment Igor is awaiting his new arm, which is a lightweight but slightly longer version which matches his other arm. The new limb is the one specifically for school. Igor helped to design it, because his greatest need is not for a cosmetically realistic arm but for one which will anchor his exercise book to the table when he is writing. He is also due to receive his third pair of custom-built boots. One will be a size eight and the other a nine, to accommodate his super-long big toe, which is forcing his foot out at an awkward angle. Barbara is trying to encourage Igor to avoid coasting along on his push-car, because he needs to build up the muscles in his tiny legs.

Igor is happy at William Cobbett County Junior School, where he will remain until he is eleven years old, but in the next few years Victor will have to carefully consider Igor's future education. He hopes to send him to a private school where he can retain the independence which has so far been the key to his survival. Such a school would enable him to have more individual tuition in smaller classes, as well as giving him the opportunity for a broader education. Victor expects him to go on to university, and Barbara feels certain his future career lies in the world of computing or languages.

Igor's home is with Barbara and Roy for as long as he wants. He goes riding every Friday and swimming on Wednesdays. He is a Cub Scout and has been camping with his pack. He continues to ignore the physical differences between himself and other children, but there is an inescapable contrast: Igor faces an uncertain future. The top part of his little body is growing, but not the bottom part, except for the unlikely toe, which resembles ET's finger.

Doctors hope to give Igor artificial legs when he's a

teenager, but to do this they would have to amputate his flipper feet. This will be a momentous decision for Igor and is one the surgeons won't ask him to make until he is at least thirteen years old and mature enough to consider the consequences. Puberty will be a difficult enough time for Igor as he watches his contemporaries developing into manhood. It is then that his awareness of his own physical shortcomings will be most acute. And should the lower-limb surgery be unsuccessful, he will have sacrificed the mobility he already has. If it works, however, artificial legs would increase his height and make him appear better-proportioned, although it would be too ambitious for the doctors to increase his height to what is normal for his age. But there is a chance that as he grows, the bottom half of his body will be unable to support the top, and therefore his mobility will be threatened. Consequently, Igor's medical team will monitor the development of his pelvis over the next few years. If they judge it able to support the weight of Igor's growing torso this will determine his future treatment. What no doctor has yet told him is that there is a chance he may have to spend his adult life in a wheelchair. For a little boy as active as Igor, that would be devastating.

There is also the question mark hanging over Igor's future in Britain. Although Home Secretary Michael Howard indicated in his letter to Victor that the application to extend Igor's visa in 1998 will be looked upon favourably, such pledges are not watertight.

If Igor is able to remain here, his future will hold many further nail-biting episodes. Whatever happens, Victor Mizzi will honour his promise to give Igor a future. If the bureaucrats force him to return to Belarus, Victor intends to seek out a caring foster family for his protégé. But one thing is certain, wherever he lives, Igor will continue to inspire love in the people who are lucky enough to care for him.

Igor and his 'Mummy' outside their home

How You Can Help

If you have been moved by Igor's story and would like to support the continued work of Chernobyl Children Life Line, donations of money and air-miles are very gratefully received.

The charity was founded to help the children of Belarus, which received 70 per cent of the contamination from the nuclear disaster. Doctors in this impoverished republic are very experienced, but they lack resources. They give CCL every assistance in helping their children. Since 1992 the charity has shipped over 500 tonnes of humanitarian aid to Belarus, including medicines, food, toys and clothing.

Donations should be sent to:

Chernobyl Children Life Line
Courts
61 Petworth Road
Haslemere
Surrey
GU27 3AX
Tel: 01428 642523
Fax: 01428 651642

Victor Mizzi, chairman and founder of Chernobyl Children Life Line, is also always pleased to hear from volunteers who would like to be host parents. They should be prepared to invite into their homes two children for one month. Over the past four years 3,500 children aged between nine and sixteen have come on UK holidays. Sixty children have attended school for one academic year. Every week that the children stay with host families in Britain, breathing uncontaminated air and eating safe food, improves their damaged immune systems.

Dr Zolovok, director of the children's hospital in Soligorsk, says:

> Every child taken to the UK for one month is 'returned' two years of life. We are hostages to the hazardous aftermath of radiation. The future of our very race is threatened with extinction as our children, our gene pool, are seriously ill.
>
> In the midst of this tragedy we have been given hope by the people of the UK. Thank you for supporting the lives of our children.

Chernobyl Children Life Line has formed sixty links across Britain. Each link has its own committee, whose objective is to raise funds, find and vet host families. The charity bring the children over from Minsk in groups of ten, with an English-speaking university lecturer, to their catchment area. It welcomes a constant supply of new members either to raise money for the children's airfares or to welcome them into their homes. Many host families become so attached to the Belarussian children that they pay to bring them over regularly every year. Some also visit their adopted families in Belarus. CCL wants to continue to expand and create more links in all areas of the British Isles. Therefore if you think you can offer help in this way, please write and the charity will give you every assistance.

Chernobyl Children Life Line has no overheads apart from postage, stationery and phone bills. There are no salaries, so all donations go straight to the cause. The charity's intention is to help 1,000 children a year, as well as supplying the hospitals with much-needed medicine.

Igor is not the only child being given long-term support and care in Britain by CCL. The McCaffrey and the Porter families are fostering leukaemia sufferers Marina Ivanovna

Grablevskaya, aged eight, Victoria Sheleg, aged two, and thirteen-year-old Vassilly Kurbuco, who has congenital deformities.

An estimated 3,800,000 people were living in the area showered with radioactive fall-out and at least 600,000 people, including 250,000 children, received high doses. No one can predict how it will affect their health in the future. Scientists say radiation levels reached more than twelve times the safety levels in areas far outside the evacuated zone. The United Nations has described the Chernobyl disaster as an 'unprecedented laboratory for human suffering' and predicts an estimated 40,000 people worldwide will die from cancer as a result of living on the 12 million acres of contaminated land.

British neurosurgeon Jenny Haley is highly experienced but shocked by what she saw on her first trip to Belarus three years ago: 'I've never seen children born without an eye or with such grossly deformed hips in my life,' she said. 'I've seen children with small heads but these are much more severe cases.'

Dr Nica Gress, a senior health adviser to the Belarus government, is calling for mass scanning of foetuses and twice-yearly checks on schoolchildren: 'Even children who live 300 miles away from the reactor are developing chronic illnesses,' she says.

For Belarussian children coming to the UK on holiday, the experience is as exciting as for a British youngster visiting Disneyland. Most of the things we take for granted, even simple things like bubble-gum, ice-cream and videos, are new and tantalizing experiences to these deprived and grateful children. Parents write ecstatically to the British host families when their children return home, happy, healthy and laden with goodies. Here are three particularly moving letters which have been recently received by Victor.

Thank you very much for your attention to our son. During the month in England he changed not only outwardly, but

114

inwardly as well. He has become more independent and grown up. My child was operated on for a brain tumour five years ago. But the tumour was not removed. I am terrified by what awaits him in the future, there are no drugs for his form of tumour. The only rescue is clean air and food. But we have neither. I am convinced that the month spent in England is very beneficial to him. This month left me with hope that there are many kind people on our planet who care about my son, just as I do.

From the Boshachevski family

Thanks a lot for taking care of our children. Our son Anton returned home in good health. He got stronger and weighs four kilogrammes more now. Frankly speaking we worried greatly when Anton was not at home for a month and so far away. But when we met him at the airport we understood that everything was fine. Anton was very happy in his English family. Every day he tells us something interesting about his trip. How wonderful it is that there are such people in your country who help the children of Belarus.

From the Somokish family

English people with their love and care help to return health to our children, and give us mothers both moral and material support. It's very important to know that there are persons who try to make our pain easier. We can almost believe all the problems will be disappeared and our son will be healed and we'll be happy together. Kostya came back in better condition and good spirit. His blood analysis shows better results now. I could never manage our problems alone. Here Kostya often feels bad and catches cold. After visiting England he gets new forces to resist diseases. It's impossible to express gratitude to people who help our children to survive. There are not a lot of people who may and want to share other's pain. In January, in Kostya's brain new swelling was found. We hope this is not a cancer swelling. We don't know yet. I hope this will be clarified after examination. Then we'll be able to make some plans for the future. Thank you, nice people.

From the Orlov family.

For the sympathetic families who devote their time and energy to helping these tragic children who live so far away, such grateful and emotive letters make it all worthwhile.

Chernobyl Children Life Line, Charity Reg: 1014278,
Inland Revenue: XN 88971

Bibliography

Chernobyl and Nuclear Power in the USSR, David Marples (Macmillan)

Truth About Chernobyl, Grigorii Medvedev (Tauris)

Children of Chernobyl: Human Cost of the World's Worst Nuclear Disaster, Adi Roche (Fount)

The Republic of Belarus: Nine Years After Chernobyl, Situation, Problems, Actions Semeshko and Antsypov (Ministry for Emergencies and Population Protection from the Chernobyl Catastrophe)

Children and Women of Belarus: Today and Tomorrow (CEE/CIS Baltic States Section, Unicef)

Chernobyl: The Forbidden Truth, Taroshinskaya and Sallabank (Carpenter)